100 Ideas for Primary Teachers

Transition to Secondary School

Molly Potter

B L O O M S B U R Y

LONDON • NEW DELHI • NEW YORK • SYDNEY

Bloomsbury Education

An imprint of Bloomsbury Publishing Plc

50 Bedford Square   1385 Broadway
London   New York
WC1B 3DP   NY 10018
UK   USA

www.bloomsbury.com

Bloomsbury is a registered trade mark of Bloomsbury Publishing Plc

First published 2015

British Library Cataloguing-in-Publication Data
A catalogue record for this book is available from the British Library.

ISBN: PB: 9781472910707
ePub: 9781472910721
ePDF: 9781472910714

Library of Congress Cataloging-in-Publication Data
A catalog record for this book is available from the Library of Congress.

10 9 8 7 6 5 4 3 2 1

Typeset by Newgen Knowledge Works (P) Ltd., Chennai, India
Printed by CPI Group (UK) Ltd, Croydon, CR0 4YY

This book is produced using paper that is made from wood grown
in managed, sustainable forests. It is natural, renewable and
recyclable. The logging and manufacturing processes conform
to the environmental regulations of the country of origin.

To view more of our titles please visit www.bloomsbury.com

Contents

Acknowledgements

I would first and foremost like to thank my ex-colleague Anna Sims who I worked extensively with on the topic of transition to secondary school when I was part of the Norfolk Healthy Schools team. Anna was great to work with and exceptionally good at crossing my t's and dotting my i's!

I would also like to thank the children in several of the schools I have worked in for allowing me to trial various PSHE ideas on them! These include pupils from Blackdale Middle School, George White Junior School, Taverham Junior School and Freethorpe Primary School. These trials were invaluable for developing many of my ideas for supporting pupils with the transition from primary to secondary school.

I need to thank Wesley Perkins for his training in the social norms approach which gave me great insights into peer influence and effective health education, and Jo Adams for her excellent training which included exploration of why it can be difficult and how to make it easier to say no.

I would also like to thank my daughter Maddy and her friends who put up with a bombardment of questions about their experiences of both transferring to and arriving at secondary school. I am sure I am an irritating and embarrassing parent!

Lastly, but by no means least-ly, I need to thank my long suffering husband Andy (the great man behind the woman) for his practical and emotional support and regular tea-provision during my intensive times of 'creation'.

Introduction

Moving from primary school to secondary school can be a big deal for children. In this transition, pupils move from a relatively nurturing environment into one where they have to fend a lot more for themselves. They are required to be more independent and to take on greater responsibility and this can all seem quite daunting. The move to secondary school also happens around the other transition time of puberty where pupils no longer think of themselves as children, yet they are far from being fully adult. This chapter in a pupil's life can be quite a difficult time to navigate. Fortunately, in recent years, this has been acknowledged and primary and secondary schools make an effort to support pupils through this testing process. However, there is always more that could be done!

That is where this book comes in. This book is filled with ideas and activities that not only support the transition of pupils from primary to secondary school, but also address a lot of the significant issues that affect this age group. While it is unlikely that anyone would carry out all of the activities in this book, many could be used to develop the PSHE curriculum for the final year at primary school. You could go even further and use the activities and ideas in this book so that pupils produce a transition project. This could result in a folder full of advice and ideas for how to navigate moving school (and many of the other issues that affect pupils at this time). This folder could be taken home by pupils for future reference.

If you are the teacher of a class at the top end of primary, or if you are responsible for transition work in your school – this book is for you. The activities and ideas can be used to create an extremely effective transition package for your pupils that will thoroughly prepare them for their move to secondary school.

How to use this book

This book includes quick, easy, practical ideas for you to dip in and out of, to support pupils in the transition from primary to secondary school.

Each idea includes:

- A catchy title, easy to refer to and share with your colleagues.
- A quote from a teacher or student describing their experiences of the idea that follows or a problem they may have had that using the idea solves.
- A summary of the idea in bold, making it easy to flick through the book and identify an idea you want to use at a glance.
- A step-by-step guide to implementing the idea.

Each idea also includes one or more of the following:

Teaching tip

Some extra advice on how or how not to run the activity or put the strategy into practice.

Taking it further

Ideas and advice for how to extend the idea or develop it further.

Bonus idea ★

There are 36 bonus ideas in this book that are extra exciting and extra original.

Involving parents

Advice for how to work with parents and carers.

Online resources also accompany this book. When the link to the resource is referenced in the book, logon to www.bloomsbury.com/100ideas-primary-transition to find the extra resources, catalogued under the relevant idea number.

Share how you use these ideas in the classroom and find out what other teachers have done using **#100ideas**.

Gathering information

Part 1

Peek at a week

"Pupils nearly always think the school day at secondary school will be completely different from primary school."

Get hold of a timetable for a typical week in the first year at secondary school. Copy and share the timetable with pupils to help them visualise what a week in their new school will be like.

Teaching tip

Registration/tutor group, citizenship, learning to learn, philosophy, pottery, theatre skills and new languages are some examples of subjects that might be found on a secondary timetable that are not on a primary one. Science might be split into physics, chemistry and biology, and design and technology might be split into different subjects.

Primary school children often learn about secondary school from older siblings and their friends. This can lead to a sense that the lessons will be completely different, the school day will be a lot longer and there will be many new subjects. Getting hold of an actual timetable for the first year at secondary school will help pupils picture what a day at their new school will be like.

- Secondary schools often have a member of staff in charge of transition. Find out who this is and ask them for a copy of a typical week's timetable for the first year. Ask for the times of lessons and breaks to be included.
- Show this timetable to your pupils and compare it to a typical day at primary school. Highlight that maths, English, science and several other lessons that happen at primary school still happen regularly at secondary school.
- Ask pupils to look for lessons that they do not have at primary school and clarify what they are.
- Look at the timings and highlight the fact that there are still breaks and lunchtimes and that the working day is about the same length as it is at primary school.
- Ask pupils to comment on the similarities and differences.

Map it

"The school is so much bigger than I am used to. I am terrified of getting lost."

Secondary schools nearly always issue their new pupils with a map of the school. Get hold of one of these maps and let pupils take a good look at it before they even visit the school.

The issue of getting lost in a much larger school is always a concern for children starting secondary school. Of course the anticipation is worse than the reality; most pupils grasp the layout of their new school within a week or two. However, the worry is real for primary pupils; some fun with a map of their new school will give them a basic picture of the site.

- Hand each pupil a copy of the map, and check they understand any labels on it.
- Mark north on the map and ask pupils which side of the school gets the sunrise and which gets the sunset.
- Ask pupils to give each other directions from one place in the school to another (for example, from the science block to the PE hall) and see if they arrive at the same place.
- Ask pupils to colour-code places on the map as those they think they will like and those they believe they won't like. Discuss pupils' reasons for colouring their map in the way they have.
- Get pupils to cut the map up into a ten-piece jigsaw and see if a friend can reassemble the map.
- Ask pupils to study the map. Then remove the map and ask pupils questions about the positions of different rooms.

Teaching tip

If pupils are going to several different secondary schools, try to get a map from each school. Ask pupils to pair up with someone who is attending a different school and list the similarities and differences that they can find about the schools from the maps.

Taking it further

Ask the secondary school where new pupils go when they first arrive, so that pupils can locate it on their maps.

Clear up lunchtime

"Where do you eat packed lunches? Where are the dining halls? Are there different canteens? Is different food served in different places? How do you pay?"

Secondary school lunchtimes can seem confusing to a child who does not know the sites, choices, routines or procedures. Finding out about this relatively unstructured time can help pupils prepare for it.

A primary school lunchtime is usually straightforward and there are always adults to help the pupils if they have any difficulties. Primary school children sense that lunchtime at secondary school is likely to be a bit different and that they will need to fend for themselves a little more.

- Ask the secondary school to give details of all lunchtime options, including where packed lunches are allowed to be eaten.
- Ask for menus and prices.
- Find out all the pay options. Some schools use hi-tech credit systems that parents/ carers can pay into in advance, alongside accepting cash.
- Ask your pupils to consider which options they are likely to choose for their lunch and what this choice will mean in terms of money and where they will spend their lunchtime.
- Ask the secondary school what pupils typically do in their lunch break after they have finished eating.
- At some secondary schools it is possible for children to avoid healthy options all week. Ask pupils to develop a healthy eating strategy for secondary school and set themselves some targets, for example, 'I will eat a piece of fruit every break time.'

Taking it further

Some secondary schools make provisions for snacks at break times. Find out if a school has a tuck shop or vending machines and what can be bought at these.

Just the register

"Does the teacher that takes the register just take the register?"

Secondary school pupils have lots of different teachers, but their registration teacher usually has some kind of pastoral care responsibility for his or her pupils. It can help pupils to know this before they get to secondary school.

The role of the form tutor varies from school to school. It is useful for pupils to know exactly what responsibilities this person has towards them. If possible, find out the answers to the following questions and share this information with pupils.

- Do pupils keep the same form tutor for the entire time they attend the school?
- How long do pupils spend with their form tutors each day and each week?
- Is it always the form tutor that parents or carers contact first with queries?
- Does the form tutor have a teaching role during registration? (Sometimes form tutors teach PSHE and citizenship, thinking skills activities or discuss current affairs with their forms.)
- Does the form tutor know how well a pupil is doing across the curriculum? Do they keep an eye on the progress the pupils in their form are making?
- Does the form tutor issue messages to pupils every morning?
- Is it the form tutor who receives letters, forms and any money for trips etc. when they are returned to school?
- Is the form tutor someone that a pupil can turn to if they are having difficulties?
- Does the form tutor take the pupils to assemblies; how often are assemblies?

Bonus idea

Ask the secondary schools that your pupils will be attending to send a photograph and a few basic and/or entertaining details about any teacher that will be a form tutor for the new intake.

Dreaded homework

"You always get tonnes and tonnes of homework at secondary school, and it takes hours and hours to do."

The perceived volume and difficulty of homework at secondary schools often causes anxiety with pupils about to leave primary school. This true or false quiz will help them to put their worries into perspective.

Primary pupils always anticipate that secondary school work, especially homework, will mean an increase in magnitude and difficulty the moment they arrive. In reality this is not the case, but curbing this belief can be hard. Of course homework will become more difficult and increase in amount, but it will do so in line with pupils' capabilities over their remaining school years.

Help pupils tackle their anxiety by producing an entertaining true or false quiz about secondary school homework – with ridiculous exaggerations. For example, here are some statements that won't be true.

- Arthur Whizzbottle from _____ school was set some maths homework in 1966 that he is still completing.
- Once you get to secondary school, you will have so much homework that you will no longer have time to sleep.
- Many first-years are set the homework of getting to the moon on their first day.
- If you hand in your homework late, you are fed to crocodiles.
- At secondary school, teachers deliberately set impossible homework because they think this is a really funny thing to do.

Smooth the move

"Secondary schools do a lot more these days to help their new pupils with transition."

Since Ofsted pointed out that pupils made little or no progress when they first arrived at secondary school, more is being done to help pupils with this transition. Find out or, better still, influence what the secondary school does to support transition.

Find out which of the following are on offer.

- Open days with exciting sample lessons.
- Information about timetables, homework, school clubs, equipment, pastoral support, personal storage of possessions, lunchtime, uniform, etc.
- Opportunities to meet and get to know new teachers.
- Opportunities to meet pupils from other primary schools who will also be attending the secondary school.
- 'Alternative brochures' and guides to moving schools written by first-year secondary pupils.
- Opportunities to meet secondary pupils and/or allocate them as mentors, including question and answer sessions, guided tours, presentations and/or leaflets made by older pupils about secondary school life.
- Activities that help pupils orientate themselves around their new school, for example, scavenger hunts, or treasure hunts.
- Opportunities for new intake pupils to spend some time in the school before the existing pupils return for term.
- Parents evenings where parents/carers can look round the school, meet staff and ask questions.

Teaching tip

Secondary schools nearly always have a teacher who is in charge of managing the transition from their catchment primary schools. Find out who this person is and make contact. Once you have direct contact, you can communicate pupils' and parents'/carers' concerns or questions as they arise.

Extracurricular clubbing

"My big sister went to photography club! She got to do some amazing projects."

A way of getting pupils excited about secondary school is to find out about extracurricular opportunities and clubs. Whet pupils' appetites by finding out exactly what happens in each club.

Secondary schools are invariably larger than primary schools; they have more staff and a greater selection of equipment. Consequently, they have many more extracurricular opportunities. Obtain a list of clubs available to pupils in their first year (these can often be found on the school website) and share it with pupils. If possible, obtain more details about each club such as when and where it takes place, who runs it, a brief description of the activities and any extra equipment that pupils need. Ask pupils to answer and discuss:

- Which three extracurricular activities would they most like to try and why?
- Which sport club would they be mostly likely to join?
- What do they feel they would gain by belonging to a club?
- What interests them about a particular club?
- What would be fun about joining a club? (For example, clubs are more relaxed than lessons, you spend time with a teacher in a less formal situation, and you will be motivated because you are doing something you enjoy or something that interests you.)
- What are the benefits of committing to any activity? (For example, you get pleasure and confidence from being good at things.)

Bonus idea ★

Extracurricular activities broadly fall into two categories: sport and creative activities. Ask pupils to decide whether they think they would most like to do sport or something creative. Discuss and explore pupil's motivations and beliefs (and possible prejudices) about taking part in their preferred and non-preferred type of activity.

Who do I go to?

"At primary school you mostly just go to your class teacher for everything – if you want the answer to a question, if you are upset, if you feel unwell or if you want permission to do something. Without one main teacher, how will I know who to go to for different kinds of help?"

Accessing the help of an adult at primary school is straightforward: you ask your class teacher, the teacher on playground duty or the midday supervisor, and they are usually very easy to find. At secondary school, this is a little less straightforward. Find out the different support available to pupils at secondary school and how they can access it, and share this information with your pupils.

Gather up information from secondary school about the following.

- Who would a pupil turn to if they were having difficulties keeping on top of their school work or homework?
- Who would a pupil report to if they were being bullied or if they were aware that someone else was being bullied?
- Where would a pupil go during the school day if they felt unwell or if they had any medical needs?
- Where would a pupil go if they had forgotten their lunch or PE kit and they needed to contact home for someone to drop it into school?
- Where would a pupil go if difficulties arose during break or lunchtimes?
- Who will deal with a pupil who is having behavioural difficulties?
- Who do pupils give letters, money or forms to when they arrive at school?
- How does a pupil access the school council and/or senior management team to put forward suggestions?

Teaching tip

Stress the idea that if pupils ever find themselves in a situation they feel they cannot sort out themselves that it is important to ask for help; asking for help is the intelligent thing to do. Also, explain that if the first person they ask cannot help, it is important to keep asking people until someone actually provides the help and support they need.

Taking it further

Get pupils to make a leaflet called 'where to find help at secondary school' including the information you have shared with them.

So many new teachers. . .

"Having so many different teachers can be quite a culture shock for pupils when they first arrive at secondary school."

After having predominantly one teacher every day at primary school, experiencing different teachers for different subjects is a significant change for pupils arriving at secondary school. There will be a lot of new adult faces for them to get to know. To aid the adjustment to this change, ask the secondary school to provide photos and basic information about some of the teachers pupils will encounter in their first year.

Taking it further

Explore the different relationship between a primary school class teacher and the subject teachers at secondary school (for example, pupils spend less time with secondary teachers, and the teachers' main focus will be the subject they are teaching, some discipline, and setting and receiving homework).

Bonus idea ★

Ask pupils to consider a typical week by looking at a timetable (see Idea 1 – Peek at a week) and consider how often they would see their English teacher, their maths teacher, their PE teacher and so on.

Most pupils know that they will have different teachers for different curriculum subjects at secondary school, but few will have considered what this will actually be like and how it differs from their experience at primary school. Exposing pupils to a photo and some information about several of the teachers they will encounter in their first year at secondary school can help to conceptualise this in a pleasant way, and give them a few familiar faces to look out for in the early weeks (which will help them to settle in).

Some secondary school websites or brochures include photos and basic information about some of their staff, which could be used to start to familiarise pupils with their new teachers. If this is not the case, ask the secondary schools to provide this information. (This could even be put together by first-year secondary pupils as part of an alternative brochure.)

No to bullying!

"Another – usually exaggerated – fear of going to secondary school is that of bullying. Kids assume there is a lot more bullying at secondary school and some perceive that it is inevitable."

If you ask any group of upper primary school children what they fear about going to secondary school, bullying will be in the top three. Pupils need to understand that secondary schools take bullying very seriously. Find out about secondary schools' anti-bullying policies and share some key information from them with your pupils.

Every school has procedures for reporting, preventing and tackling bullying. These procedures are usually documented, either in an anti-bullying policy or as part of a behaviour policy. Ask the secondary schools that your pupils will attend for a copy of their anti-bullying policy, or to answer the questions below.

- How does the school define bullying?
- How does the school encourage pupils to report bullying (either if they are a target of bullying or if they have witnessed it)?
- Who in the school can bullying be reported to?
- What happens when incidents of bullying are reported?
- How does the school make sure that the bullying has stopped?
- Is there someone in the school who has the role of monitoring incidents of bullying and how they are dealt with?
- Does the school do anything during the annual anti-bullying week?

Share the answers to these questions with your pupils.

The 'anti-bullying' section of this book (Part 4) has more information, advice and activities on this topic.

Involving parents

Ask pupils to make some entertaining true and false quizzes about bullying and anti-bullying procedures to take home and test their parents' knowledge of bullying.

Taking it further

Most secondary schools do something in anti-bullying week. You could ask the secondary school to get their pupils to provide anti-bullying information specifically aimed at reassuring your primary school pupils.

Skool rools

"Believe it or not, kids actually like rules. They make expectations clear and make things fair. But that does not mean that every student will adhere to all the rules all of the time!"

Secondary schools do not always publicise their school rules, but there are always expectations relating to uniform, attendance, completing work, treatment of others, items not allowed in school and safety. If possible, obtain a list of the secondary school's rules, expectations and/or behaviour policy (sometimes these can be found in the school brochure) and share some key information with pupils.

Going to secondary school can cause anxiety because there are so many changes and so many unknowns. Primary school children have a perception that secondary schools are stricter, but getting hold of the secondary rules and/or expectations will usually show that there is little difference from primary school rules.

Spend some time looking at the rules and explore the reasons for each one. Rules are always more palatable, and therefore more likely to be followed, if the reasoning behind them is understood. This usually falls broadly into three categories: safety, optimising learning and respect for others.

Help pupils to understand that secondary schools have potentially hazardous equipment (for example, chemicals, Bunsen burners, technology tools), and this means that strict safety rules must be followed. Make pupils aware that some individual teachers will also have subject-specific rules relating to safety (for example, in science laboratories, technology rooms and sports halls).

See if there are any additional rules at secondary school compared with primary, and explore why this might be.

Bonus idea ★

Pupils have more unsupervised time at secondary school than at primary school (for example, during breaks and moving between different lessons). At these times there are less likely to be adults around to enforce rules. Discuss with your pupils how they feel about this and any concerns this might cause.

You're in trouble!

"All the teachers are stricter at secondary school and you are far more likely to get punished for things. Pupils are always being given detentions."

Nearly every secondary school has some kind of punitive measure, such as detentions or behaviour marks, which work effectively to prevent most pupils from misbehaving. It can be helpful for pupils to know what these procedures are before they go to secondary school.

Contact the secondary school(s) your pupils will attend and find out their behaviour management strategies and systems. Also find out what punitive measures the school uses, how they are issued and for what, as well as what rewards the school uses. Share this information with your pupils.

Consider behaviour management with your class by discussing the following questions.

- Why does a school need punishments like detentions?
- Do you think punishments work?
- If you were in charge of a school, how would you help pupils to behave well?
- Do you think secondary schools need to do more or less than primary schools to help their pupils behave?
- What helps you to behave well?
- What prevents you from behaving well?
- What is the impact of bad behaviour?
- Do you think rewards or punishments are better at getting pupils to behave?
- Why do you think pupils misbehave?
- At secondary school, teachers see their pupils for less time than at primary school. Do you think this makes it easier or harder for secondary school teachers to manage behaviour?

> **Involving parents**
>
> Find out if the secondary school has a procedure for informing parents or carers when their child misbehaves or does not do what is expected. Share this information with pupils and parents.

13

First day nerves

"As the first day at secondary school looms near, some pupils will start to feel really nervous. It's important to make this day run as smoothly as it can to give pupils a good start."

Most secondary schools ensure that pupils know exactly where to go on their first day. Once pupils are there, they are given a lot of information — possibly too much to take in all at once. Find out as much as you can about this first day so that you can spread the burden of 'information overload' and help pupils feel less anxious.

Consider how daunting the very first day at secondary school might be. Find out some information about this first day to help your pupils settle in. Many secondary schools finalise details like timetables and class teachers close to the end of the school year, so some of this information will only be available around June or July. To help with first day nerves, ask the secondary school(s) about the points below.

- Where pupils will go when they first arrive (this could be shown on a map) and what they need to bring.
- How much of the first day will be a general introduction and how many lessons the pupils will actually go to.
- What will be demonstrated on the first day, for example, lunchtime procedures, where pupils can go at break times, home communication systems, etc.
- As much practical information as possible, for example, amount of homework in the first week, how this will be set and handed in, will pupils be forgiven for being late to classes at first, will they need to fill in any forms or bring any information, will they need to set up anything for lunchtimes (for example, payment).

Taking it further

Using the information you have shared with them ask pupils to list the things that will happen on their first day of secondary school. Start off with practical things but then encourage pupils to think about other experiences like meeting new friends, new teachers, new route to school, feeling nervous. Ask pupils to reflect on which bits they are looking forward to and which bits they feel unsure of and discuss these.

Try out topics

"It's a good idea to get pupils interested in the actual work they will be covering at secondary school."

A great way to get pupils enthused about the work they will be covering at secondary school is to find out some of the topics they will study in the first term. Explore these topics to stimulate pupils' interest and help them visualise the kind of work they will be doing.

Ask a contact at the secondary school to list some topics that are covered in the first year. The subjects that lend themselves best to this include history, geography, science, PSHE and citizenship, and English (sometimes English is topic-based at secondary school).

Obviously you will not want to cover any of the topics in great detail, but you could start to encourage pupils' curiosity in one of the following ways. Ask pupils to:

- Draw a spider diagram displaying what they already know about a topic.
- Do an internet search to find ten interesting facts on a topic.
- Create quizzes on a topic for the class to answer.
- Imagine that they were going to teach this topic – how would they get pupils interested?
- Sort facts from different topics into the correct topics.
- Produce an advert 'selling' a topic to other pupils using persuasive language and pictures.
- Produce a freeze-frame relating to a particular topic; classmates can guess what is happening.

Involving parents

Get pupils to investigate what the adults at home know about a particular topic and bring in any facts that are shared.

Older and wiser

"Don't forget, pupils who have been through the transition to secondary school are a fantastic resource."

Getting advice from existing first-year secondary pupils is a very effective way to reassure primary school pupils about transition and life at the new school. Work with your secondary school to gather up some of this advice.

One of the most reassuring activities is to collect and deliver advice from existing secondary pupils. Your primary pupils will be really eager to hear what they have to say. Addressing these questions will provide pupils with much-needed reassurance:

- What did you find most difficult about going to secondary school and do you still find this difficult?
- How long did it take before secondary school felt normal?
- Is there anything that scares you about being at secondary school?
- In what ways is secondary school better than primary school?
- How long did it take before you knew your way around the school?
- Is bullying a big problem?
- What do you really enjoy?
- Do you have a lot more homework?
- Do you find the lessons difficult?
- What do you do with your form tutor?
- Are there adults you can turn to if you are having difficulties?
- What do you think of your teachers?
- What are the main differences between primary and secondary school?
- What advice would you give to a pupil who had just arrived at secondary school who was feeling really nervous?

Positive change

Part 2

Celebrate good times!

"Lots of schools have a celebration of some kind when their top year group moves on to secondary school."

Moving from primary to secondary school is a significant transition. While it is important to help pupils anticipate the move positively, it's also a good idea to mark the end of primary school with a celebration and/or reflection.

As pupils near the end of their time at primary school, use one of the following ideas to mark the occasion.

An event
- 'Which teacher?' . . .' – gather up pupils' memories of their primary school teachers and turn some of them into a humorous quiz.
- 'I remember . . .' – let pupils share their best memories of primary school.
- 'Fascinating things I learnt' – let pupils share their learning memories.

An exhibition, including:
- lists of pupils' top five memories of primary school
- memorable things that teachers said
- photos
- descriptions of memorable lessons or assemblies
- poems that sum up a pupil's experience at primary school
- timelines depicting the journey through primary school
- hopes, wishes and dreams for the future
- a memory map – a plan of the school with site-specific memories marked on it.

Taking it further

Many primary schools have traditions for saying goodbye to their pupils at the end of primary school, but why not ask the school council what they think would be the best way to do this.

Bonus idea ★

Produce keepsakes that the pupils can take away with them, for example, booklets containing memories and photos, or cards that teachers and fellow pupils can write in.

The Change Curve

"The emotions that occur around change can be like a roller coaster!"

The Change Curve shows a typical emotional response to changes when they happen. Share the Change Curve with your pupils and use it to initiate discussions about how change affects us.

Explain that the curve (see online resources) shows an emotional reaction to a big change. Ensure pupils understand what the axes represent (X = time and Y = positive and negative emotion) and give them time to understand it.

Next, ask pupils to work in pairs and discuss the following questions.

- In what way can the start of a change feel exciting? (It can be thrilling anticipating new experiences).
- What do you think causes a delay in a negative emotional response? (It takes a while to take everything in.)
- What is it about change that can knock people's confidence and make them feel unsettled? (Going into the unknown can feel unsafe for a while and it is hard to feel confident when you are getting used to new things.)
- What do you think will help you when you are in the 'slump' of the graph? (Talk to people you trust, know that you won't feel like this for long.)
- How long do you think it will take you to get to the end of this graph after you have arrived at secondary school?

Taking it further

Discuss the idea that some people are wired up to worry more than others. Ask pupils to work in pairs and ask each other questions to investigate whether they worry more or less than their partner. The starting point is to find out what their partner worries about.

Before and after

"Change can make you very anxious before it happens but a couple of weeks after the change has passed you can look back and wonder what all the fuss was about!"

Some people deal with change better than others, but there is nearly always an emotional response. Managing this response makes the difference between a relatively smooth journey and a turbulent one. Help pupils put change in perspective by exploring their experience of change in the past.

Ask pupils to write down a change they have experienced in the past (for example, moving to a new class, moving house, having a different teacher, starting a new club or activity). Next ask them to answer the following questions about the change.

- How long before the change did you know that it was going to happen?
- Did you have any worries about the change and if so what were they?
- Were you looking forward to anything about the change?
- When did you start to have feelings about the impending change?
- How long after the change had happened did you start to feel settled?

Discuss pupils' answers as a whole class, including the following points.

- Worry is an unhelpful thought that goes round and round in your head.
- Telling yourself that any new situation will feel 'normal' after a short while can help prevent worry.
- Before and during any change can be the hardest part, because there are still lots of unknowns at this point.
- After the change, you know what you are dealing with and can start to adjust.

Taking it further

Ask pupils to draw a Change Curve (Idea 17) showing their emotions over the time from before, during and after the change they explored. They could draw a line to show times when they felt positive emotions and negative emotions, then label what happened to make them feel this way. Hopefully, most pupils' timelines will demonstrate that they soon felt comfortable about what had changed.

Worry worry

"Worrying can be really unhelpful, especially if you are worrying about something inevitable, like going to secondary school."

Some people are simply wired up to worry more than others. Some pupils will worry a lot about going to secondary school and others will give it little thought and accept things as they come. Helping pupils to understand and manage worry is useful generally, but also to specifically help with the transition to secondary school.

We tend to worry about things in the future that have some uncertainty and unknowns; these situations can make us not trust ourselves to cope. Secondary school is potentially full of unknowns for pupils and can therefore cause a lot of worry.

Ask pupils to work in pairs or small groups and discuss answers to the following questions. (Some possible example answers have been given.)

1 What is worry? (Worrying could be defined as an unhelpful thought going round and round in your head.)
2 What kind of things can cause a person to worry? (Changes in the future, doing something you regret, believing you won't cope.)
3 Does worry ever achieve anything good? (No. Do not confuse worry with fear — fear has its uses to avoid dangers!)
4 Does worrying change what happens in the future in any way? (It makes you dread the future and be more cautious).
5 What would help someone who was really worried about secondary school? (Find out as much information about secondary school as they can; talk to older children who are already at secondary school; relaxation.)

Teaching tip

Some general tips to help deal with worry are to talk it through with someone, tell the unhelpful thought to go away, remember that after a short while everything will feel settled again, imagine yourself really enjoying a new situation.

Taking it further

Ask pupils to create a poster that aims to help people understand and deal with worry. Alternatively, ask pupils to respond to an agony aunt letter where a pupil explains that s/he is really worried about going to secondary school.

Strange change?

"We ask pupils to deal with a huge amount of change when they go to secondary school. Change can be extremely unsettling – and for some more than others."

Change is inevitable. Dealing with change is about managing thoughts and emotions when moving from the 'known' into the 'unknown'. Take time – perhaps in a PSHE lesson – to explore the pros and cons of change in the context of moving to secondary school.

Involving parents

Send home a sheet that prompts discussion between pupils and their parents/carers about the changes the pupils will experience. List the changes and ask pupils to write how they feel about each one. Get pupils to take this home and discuss each change with the adults at home. Ask pupils to write at least two sentences about the discussion they had.

Discuss change – initially in general terms and then the specific change involved in moving to secondary school – to help pupils investigate their own feelings about change and transition.

To explore the issue of change generally, list some changes that happen in people's lives, for example, a new hairstyle, moving house in the same city/town, moving to another part of the country, learning to swim, having a birthday and being older, a good friend moving away, being given a new dinner that you have never had before, having to do more jobs around the house to get your pocket money, and, of course, going up to secondary school.

Ask pupils to develop some scoring criteria to judge how big a change is. For example:

- how often you come across or spend time thinking about the new situation
- how the new situation makes you feel compared with the old situation
- what is good and bad about the new situation
- how different the new situation is from the old
- how much you knew about the change before it happened.

Ask pupils to order the changes from smallest to biggest – this will stimulate a lot of discussion!

Ask pupils to discuss the following questions.

- When change happens, are you more likely to worry about it before, during or after the actual change?
- What is difficult about change?
- What helps people cope with change?
- In what ways can change be good?
- What advice would you give somebody about dealing with change?

To explore the change of moving from primary to secondary school, give pupils a list of the changes that happen when pupils move to secondary school, such as having a new journey to school and making new friends. Ask pupils to put the changes into three piles:

- Changes I am looking forward to.
- Changes I am worried about.
- Changes that I am not sure how I feel about!

Ask pupils to pair up and discuss the reasons for putting each change on the pile they did, then discuss the actual changes as a whole class. You can bring the following helpful points into the discussion.

- Try and stay positive about the move. Focus on the things you are looking forward to more than the things that make you worry.
- Realise that all change brings about opportunities.
- Everyone will be given lots of information about secondary school before they get there. This will mean there are not a lot of 'unknowns'.
- Change is unsettling, but it can seem worse in anticipation than in reality. You will feel settled within a few weeks of starting secondary school.
- Not everything in your life will change. Home will stay the same, some friends will still be in the same classes, etc.

Taking it further

Ask pupils to think about a change that has happened in their own lives. Ask them to rate how big they thought the change was from 0 to 10, then complete a timeline showing how they felt at the different times before, during and after the change.

23

On the grapevine

"A great deal of pupils' worries come from exaggerated rumours about secondary school. These rumours need to be challenged!"

The rumour about new kids getting their heads flushed down toilets has been around for aeons! Sadly, many pupils can't rely upon older siblings to dispel these myths. Explore what pupils think about secondary school so you can challenge any exaggerations or lies!

In the centre of some large sheets of flipchart paper write the following words:

- Homework
- Older students
- The journey to school
- Teachers
- Lessons
- A bigger school site/building
- Friends
- Extras – anything that happens at secondary school that does not happen at primary school.

Spread the sheets out and invite pupils to write on them, expressing how they feel and/or what they think about each heading at secondary school.

Collect up the sheets when most pupils have stopped writing. Use each sheet to stimulate discussions about issues at secondary school. Challenge any exaggerations and lies, and highlight any positives. Also be sure to tackle the particular rumours of:

- older children bullying younger children (there have been no reported incidents of heads being flushed down toilets)
- huge amounts of difficult homework set every day (not the case)
- pupils getting lost being a big problem (by the end of the first or second week, pupils will know exactly where to go).

How do you feel?

"Pupils will be worried about different aspects of the transition and have different perceptions from each other depending on what they themselves have heard about secondary school!"

Look at a comprehensive list of the actual changes that happen when a pupil gets to secondary school. Use it to find out how pupils feel about each individual change.

Create a table that has the changes that occur when a pupil goes to secondary school in the first column and a variety of ways of feeling along the first row. Leave a few blank rows for pupils to add their own changes.

Examples to put along the first row include: excited, don't like, OK, worried, not sure, great, sad, angry, scared, confused, etc.

Give each pupil a copy of the table and ask them to tick the words that represent how they feel about each change.

Use the tables to gauge individual responses to each of the changes. They could be completed anonymously, or you could ask pupils to put their name on the table but complete it without letting anyone else see their answers. This way answers will not be influenced by their peers.

Use the results to find out what the big issues are about transition for your class.

Taking it further

You could use the results of this activity to inform parents/carers and staff at secondary school about what is concerning pupils when it comes to transition. Pupil concerns vary from year to year and from pupil to pupil.

New school resolutions

"A definite bonus for starting a new school is that it is a chance to turn over a new leaf. Fresh starts can be exciting!"

Starting at a new school is an obvious time to make resolutions or set goals. Whether pupils choose to get better at something they struggle with or to embrace new opportunities, setting goals can initiate a positive approach towards their new school.

Involving parents

Ask pupils to write their resolutions down and take them home to discuss with the adults at home. Ask them to ask their parents/carers how they could help them to achieve their resolutions, for example, show an interest, give reminders, compliment any effort they have put in to achieve their resolution.

Spend some time developing some individual goals/resolutions for each pupil in your class. Before you start, discuss what makes a person more likely to succeed with a goal or resolution. Effective resolutions:

- are worded positively
- are realistic
- are ones that pupils can imagine themselves doing
- have a clear first step to take
- are ones that pupils are prepared to put some effort into.

Pupils will have some ideas of their own about what to choose as resolutions or goals. However, if they are short of ideas, some of the following could be included.

- To get better grades in a specific subject.
- To join a club.
- To get really fit.
- To arrive at school on time every day.
- To always have the right equipment.
- To organise work more neatly.
- To focus on the things I like about school and develop a positive attitude.
- To do homework on the day it is set.
- To only say kind things about others.

Ask pupils to choose three resolutions that they think they could realistically achieve. Then ask them to pair up and discuss how they plan to succeed.

Nice to meet you

"Sending personal information to their new school ahead of themselves can make pupils already start to feel connected with their future school."

Sharing information about themselves with their new teachers is an encouraging way to support the transition to secondary school. It gives pupils an indirect way to feel listened to before they arrive.

Create a form with questions and ask pupils to complete them. You could include:

- basic details – name, birthday, star sign, nicknames, hobbies
- top three subjects at school
- least favourite subject and why
- other favourites: colour, meal, TV programme, season, animal etc.
- how you like to spend your free time
- what you are looking forward to about secondary school
- what you will miss about primary school
- a goal for secondary school (see Idea 23 – New school resolutions)
- your favourite school memory so far
- aspirations for your future – including possible occupations
- three answers to the question, 'What do you think of *<pupil>*?' with answers given by friends, teachers or family
- a self portrait
- three adjectives that describe you
- some sentences to complete:
  - School is . . .
  - Learning is . . .
  - I am happiest at school when . . .
  - Something I struggle with at school is . . .

Teaching tip

Liaise with the secondary school to produce a formatted information sheet to be completed by all primary pupils about to move the school. Forward this to the secondary school to help year group leaders and form or registration tutors familiarise themselves with their new intake.

Taking it further

When pupils get to secondary school they will meet a lot of new peers that do not know them at all. Ask pupils to think of information about themselves they will readily share with others in those first days of secondary school.

Early days

"The first day at secondary school can be overwhelming with so much new information to get your head around. You feel like you'll never remember it all."

The first few days at secondary school will involve pupils receiving a lot of information. Help pupils to realise that this will be the case and give them some handy tips for how to cope.

- Remember that the first days will be the hardest in terms of having to remember lots of things. It can only get easier.
- If you are confused about anything – just ask. Keep asking if you are still confused or you have forgotten. You don't just have teachers to ask – you can ask your new classmates too. Don't be shy!
- Write things down! Lots of secondary schools give pupils a book for homework and other details. Don't assume you will just remember – always write it down.
- It is usual to feel overwhelmed at the end of the first day and possibly the second and third. By the fourth day and beyond things will start feeling less new.
- Remember the Change Curve (Idea 17). You might feel a little wobbly at first, but there will come a point where you feel normal again!
- When adults start new jobs they can feel nervous and overwhelmed too!
- Lots of things you will have worried about before you started secondary school will soon seem silly!
- Even if other pupils look confident, they probably feel exactly the same as you.
- Teachers will forgive you if you forget a few things at first.

Sell it!

"It's important to remember that while we need to be realistic about moving to secondary school and all the changes it involves, we also need to help pupils feel positive about their new school!"

You need to acknowledge that the transition to secondary school is a big change, but there is a danger of just focusing on the things that cause worry. Don't forget to get pupils excited about it too! Use these ideas to muster up some enthusiasm for secondary school.

This activity is best done after you have completed most of your transition work, as pupils need to have a fairly good understanding about secondary school.

Ask pupils to list the changes they know they will experience at secondary school. Then ask them what the positive aspects of each change might be. Encourage pupils to use humour and exaggerate. For example:

- You will need a bigger bag and it will be heavier. The benefit is that you will become fit and strong.
- You have a new route to school. The benefit might be that you were getting bored of the old journey.
- You have lots of different teachers. The benefit is that if you don't like one, you don't have to have him or her all day.
- You will be the youngest in the school. The benefit is that no one will expect much of you!

Once all the benefits have been explored, ask pupils to create a magazine or, better still, TV advert 'selling' secondary school. Encourage pupils to make these humorous and use lots of persuasive talk!

Once pupils have looked at all the adverts, ask them to list their five favourite benefits – however ridiculous.

> **Teaching tip**
>
> Using humour in this way might seem to trivialise the issue of transition to secondary school. However, using humour can help pupils reframe their worries about moving school.

Aspirations!

"It's hard when you're a teenager to see the link between what you do at school and how it will impact your future choices."

Linking aspirations to secondary school work helps pupils focus on what they hope to get out of the last part of their schooling.

Involving parents

Send home some discussion 'homework' that asks the adults at home to list three 'hopes and dreams' for their child's future. Pupils could then be asked to comment further upon what their parents/carers said.

Bonus idea ★

Hold an aspirations day. Ask parents/carers and other adults in your school's community to come and talk to pupils about their careers. Try and represent a broad range of careers – including people who run their own businesses. Get pupils to think about the questions they would like to ask each person before they meet them. Be sure that each person makes clear what they had to do to get their job, and what they did well in at school.

This activity could be done on a small scale or a really large one. Here are three ideas to start pupils thinking about what career they might want when they grow up.

1 Introduce pupils to the idea that there are many different jobs by brainstorming (with your class) all the jobs they have heard of. Add some unusual jobs that you had previously researched and ask pupils what they think a person with this job does. Emphasise that there are so many different jobs, no one person is likely to know them all.

2 Use www.nationalcareersservice.direct.gov. uk. Ask pupils to find three jobs on the site that they think they would enjoy, and make notes about what is needed to enter each career. Link this to secondary school education and the qualifications they would need.

3 Ask pupils to prioritise the things that would be important to them about their career, for example, working with people, being their own boss, making lots of money, helping people, working alone, being in charge, making big decisions, being an expert in something, working outside, working in the same place every day, working mostly at a computer, not feeling stressed, travelling around, variety, etc.

Write to yourself!

"We can often give ourselves advice with hindsight, but how about giving our future self some advice?"

If you have done some work with your pupils that has helped them to conceptualise the move to secondary school, why not use the understanding your pupils have gained to advise their future selves?

Secondary school will probably seem a long way away, even at the point that pupils leave primary school for the summer holidays. This 'distance' will help them to be objective about the move. Get pupils to write to themselves in the future and deliver wisdom they have already collected from transition work.

Ask pupils to imagine themselves at secondary school in their first week. What will they worry about and what advice should they give themselves to help?

Here are some suggestions, but pupils are bound to have lots of ideas themselves.

- Any nervousness you feel at first will go away within a week or so.
- You will get used to everything and things will become routine quite quickly.
- A lot of things will stay the same, like home, outside school activities and family.
- Talk to someone if you feel anxious.
- If there seems like a lot to remember, don't worry, it will soon be automatic.
- Even if other pupils look confident, they probably feel exactly the same way as you do. Make the effort to be friendly and make friends.
- Secondary school needs you to be more independent. This is part of growing up. Plan and think about the day ahead, and what you need, the night before.

Involving parents

Ask pupils to take their letters home to share with their parents/carers. Suggest that they inform their parents/carers that this advice will be useful in their first week at secondary school.

Uniform all round

"I hate wearing a school uniform. My parents hated wearing it. My grandparents hated wearing it. . . ."

Most secondary schools have a school uniform and most pupils hate it! This agreement spectrum tool can evoke some interesting discussions, and might help some pupils resent uniforms a little less!

Many secondary school pupils continuously bend the rules when it comes to uniform; this can cause frequent conflicts between pupils and their teachers and parents. This idea creates a thought-provoking discussion about the pros (and cons) of school uniform.

1 Create an agreement spectrum by placing the word 'agree' at one side of the room and 'disagree' at the other.
2 Explain that you will make a statement and that pupils need to stand on the spectrum to indicate how much they agree or disagree.
3 Make one statement at a time.
4 Once everyone has decided where to stand, invite discussion by asking, 'Who would like to say anything about where they are standing?'

Use these or similar statements.

- Teenagers can be very fashion-conscious.
- Some teenagers get picked on if they are not wearing the 'right' clothes.
- School uniform takes away the decision of what to wear on a school day.
- Teenagers do not like to stand out.
- Teenagers often try to change their uniform in some way to be different.
- School uniform protects pupils from being picked on because they are not wearing the 'right' clothes.

Sets, groups and streams

"Some pupils really worry about how they will be put into ability groups for different subjects at secondary school."

Many pupils experience being set according to ability at primary school. However, a sense that secondary school is where school work and achievement becomes more important can cause pupils to worry about how they will be grouped. To help with this, explore the reasons and benefits of setting with your pupils.

Even in the most nurturing of primary schools, pupils with less academic ability will be fully aware of where they are positioned in the informal hierarchy of academic success. There is nearly always a feeling of some stigmatisation due to this. Secondary schools do not necessarily group according to ability initially, but it is likely that pupils will experience more 'streaming' in their time there overall.

Use the following questions to explore the issues of success in academic subjects and setting according to academic ability.

- What things can people be good at that are not taught in school? (People skills, being creative, making people laugh, etc.)
- What are you good at that is not taught in school?
- What kind of jobs do people who do not pass lots of exams at school go on to do?
- Would it be a sensible idea if schools gave all pupils good grades all of the time?
- Years ago, teachers gave all pupils the same work to do in every lesson. Was this a good or bad idea? Why?
- Why do you think secondary schools put pupils into sets for some lessons?
- How would someone get moved up a set?

Taking it further

Every secondary school approaches setting differently – from those that set just in maths and English to those that 'stream' the whole year group. Find out what happens in the secondary schools your pupils are going to and inform them.

Bonus idea ★

Remind pupils that there are lots of well-known people who achieved great things despite receiving bad school reports or leaving school (or university) because it did not work for them, for example, Albert Einstein, Richard Branson, Quentin Tarantino, Daniel Radcliffe, Steve Jobs.

The Bunsen burner

"Pupils will encounter a lot more equipment at secondary school than they did at primary school."

This activity goes well with Idea 37 – New subjects, and it aims to get pupils excited about the new opportunities that will come with their new school. Rouse enthusiasm by looking at some of the equipment secondary schools use!

This activity requires some preparation, but it can be entertaining!

- Ask the secondary schools for a list of equipment that pupils will use that they would not have used at primary school. This will probably be mostly science, sports and technology equipment, for example, Bunsen burners, scientific calculator, safety goggles, gym weights, etc.
- Get pictures of each piece of equipment from the internet. It would be better still if the secondary school could provide the pictures, of course! You only need about ten pictures, but it is best if there is a mixture of some obvious and some obscure pieces of equipment.
- Ask pupils to match the equipment with the lesson, and speculate when and how it is used.
- Go through each of the items and explain their use.

Ask pupils the following questions:

1 Why do you think secondary schools have more equipment than primary schools? (More equipment is needed to explore some subjects. Secondary schools have more pupils and therefore more money to spend.)
2 Are you looking forward to using new pieces of equipment?

Bonus idea ★

Ask the secondary schools to provide photographs of classrooms where different subjects are taught, and ask pupils to match each room with the subject taught in it.

Practical advice

Part 3

Visit the website

"It's easily forgotten, but the website of any school is a good place for pupils to find out information about their new school."

Every secondary school has a website. This is a brilliant resource for pupils to acquaint themselves with their new school. Issue a scavenger hunt to inspire a thorough search of the website.

Either give pupils their secondary school's website address to take home, or allocate school time to explore it. To help pupils maintain interest and explore the website extensively, ask pupils to find as many of the following as they can.

- A picture of a pupil looking happy.
- A piece of information they did not know.
- A picture of some pupils working.
- The school motto, vision, mission or purpose.
- A picture and the name of the head teacher.
- The name of another member of staff.
- The full address of the school.
- A sentence that tells you one thing that happens at the school.
- The date of the last Ofsted report.
- One piece of information about extracurricular clubs.
- A piece of recent news.
- The number of students at the school.
- An event that is going to happen at the school in the future.
- The number your parents/carers need to phone if you are ill.
- A sentence from a school policy.
- A job vacancy at the school.
- A picture of, or some information about, sports at the school.

Getting organised

"Becoming organised is a really important skill for life. Some people are naturally organised, others have to work harder at it."

As children grow up, there is an expectation that they will become more independent and be able to organise themselves. Get pupils to reflect upon how organised they are now, the need to be more organised for secondary school and how to achieve this.

Ask pupils to reflect upon how organised they currently are using the following quiz. Each 'yes' scores one point.

1 Is your bedroom mostly tidy?
2 Do you always get your homework in on time?
3 Do you always have a pen or pencil to write with at school?
4 Do you always remember what you need to take to school?
5 Is your desk or tray at school tidy now?
6 Do you hardly ever lose things?

A score of 6 = ultra organised, 5 or 4 = organised, 3 = average, and 2 or 1 = a little unorganised.

Next, ask four confident pupils to come to the front of the class. Give each pupil one of the following pieces of advice on a piece of paper, and explain that the pupils are going to give the rest of the class some tips about getting organised for secondary school – but without using words!

- Set your alarm clock so you have plenty of time to get ready for school.
- Make sure you know what time you need to leave to get to school on time.
- Pack your school bag the night before.
- Have a list of things that you need to take to school on the back of the door.

If pupils really struggle – give them some clues.

Taking it further

Discuss the reasons why parents/carers nag sometimes. Explain that nagging is not nice for the parents or the child, but it happens when someone continually fails to do something. Ask pupils to consider if they ever get nagged and think about what it is they are failing to do that causes the nagging. What could they do to prevent the nagging?

Bonus idea ★

Ask pupils to write and illustrate each piece of advice.

Healthy homework habits

"Homework can become a real chore if pupils don't develop good habits."

The amount of homework pupils receive will increase as they go through secondary school. This will not be a problem if pupils develop a routine for completing it. Explore how pupils currently approach homework, and consider good homework habits.

Involving parents

Make parents aware of the tips for good homework habits. Ask parents what they can do to support their child to complete his or her homework, for example, create a homework station, show an interest, check homework, give help if it is needed, etc.

Consider pupils' current homework habits by asking the following questions. Ask them to be honest!

1 Do you do your homework the night before it is due, the day it is set, or is it different each time?
2 Do you rely on your parents/carers to remind you to do your homework and to remember to take it back to school?
3 Do you really concentrate when you are doing your homework, or do you do it in front of the TV or somewhere where you are often distracted?
4 Do you do your homework late at night when you are really tired?
5 Do your parents/carers have to nag you to get your homework done?
6 Do you always remember when homework needs to be handed in?
7 Do you spend time procrastinating (putting off beginning your homework by constantly finding other things to do)?
8 Do you take care to do your homework as best as you can, or do you just rush it?

As a class, discuss the answers that a few pupils gave. Ask each pupil if they think their response is a good way of approaching homework. Explain that at secondary school the amount of homework will steadily increase, and that doing it last minute might mean you have a lot to do in one evening.

To consider good homework habits, describe a fictional character called Sam. She has terrible homework habits. She rarely gets her homework in on time and, when she does, it is clear she hasn't put much effort in. Ask pupils to create a poster of good homework habits to persuade Sam to approach homework in a better way.

Once pupils have completed their posters, find out how many of these tips they included. Ask for a show of hands after you read out each one. At the end, ask if anyone came up with any other tips.

- Do homework on the day it is set, or make firm plans for when to do each piece (and stick to them!).
- Make sure you know what homework has been set and when it is due in.
- Have a short break when you get home, but then get on with your homework.
- Ask an adult to check over your homework when it is finished.
- Complete homework in a place where you won't be distracted by anything.
- Have a 'homework station' with pencils, rulers, erasers and sharpeners, etc.
- Don't create excuses not to do homework – remember how good it feels to finish a good piece of work.
- Remember that starting is often the hardest bit. The sooner you start, the sooner you will finish.
- Put your homework straight into your school bag when it is finished.
- If you find a piece of homework really hard, either get an adult to help or take it into school and ask your teacher to explain what you need to do again.
- If you are struggling to concentrate, allow yourself a ten minute break.
- Never start homework close to bedtime. You won't be able to concentrate well, and you might find it difficult to get to sleep afterwards.

Taking it further

Explore the idea of procrastination with pupils. Give personal stories of procrastination. Ask: What is it? What are the signs that someone is procrastinating? What prevents people starting and/or finishing work? How can people overcome procrastination?

New routes

"An often overlooked practicality can be the impact of a new route or way of travelling to secondary school."

For the majority of pupils, moving on to secondary school will mean a new route – and possibly means – of travelling to school. This can be a big cause of worry, especially if a bus is involved. Help pupils to clarify how they will get to secondary school to alleviate any worry.

Involving parents

Advise parents/carers to do a dummy run of the new route to school/ the bus stop/walking to a friend's house etc. with their child in the summer holidays. Time how long the route takes so that pupils can be sure that they leave enough time to get to school.

Near the end of their last term at primary school, find out how pupils will be travelling to their new school: walking, cycling, bus or being dropped off. Send pupils home to find out details of how they will be getting to their new school.

- If they are walking or cycling, ask for the route they will take and how long it will take.
- If they are going by bus, ask them to find out where and when the bus leaves, how long the journey will be and where it will drop pupils off. Find out the cost, if there is one.
- If they are going by car, ask them to find out the route, who will be taking them and where they will be picked up from.

Once pupils have the details, support them with their new journey to school in the following ways.

- Ask pupils to write instructions for 'how I will get to secondary school'. They should include as much detail as possible, including the time they will need to leave, when they will arrive, the route, what they will see on the route and the means of travel. They might need to use the internet to find journey times for walking, cycling and/or driving.

- Explore the routes the walkers and the cyclists will take. Are there any particularly busy roads or dangerous crossings that could be avoided? Are they travelling the safest route?
- Consider the arrival at school. It is usually busy and crowded with lots of cars, pedestrians and cyclists. What can pupils do to ensure they arrive safely? (Where is the best place to be dropped off by a car? Where will the bus drop them off? Does the school have more than one entrance and, if so, which is the best one for each pupil to enter by?)
- Explore the idea of pupils that live in close proximity to each other sharing a lift, cycling together or walking together. Who would call for whom in the morning and at what time?
- Make it known to all pupils who will be on the bus (or buses) together so they know who to look out for.

Bonus idea

For lots of pupils the journey to school is an opportunity to get some exercise. Ask pupils how they could maximise this opportunity for all, whatever their mode of travelling is (for example, people who travel by car or bus could ask to be dropped off some distance from the school so they still have to walk a little). Ask pupils to produce posters that promote the journey to school as an opportunity to exercise.

Rules of the road

"The top end of primary school – before pupils make the move to secondary school – is a really good time to revise road safety."

Statistics show that the age group of children that have newly arrived at secondary school have an increased likelihood of being involved in road traffic accidents. For this reason, it is a really good idea to revisit road safety (preferably in a different way).

Teaching tip

It is interesting to note that the reasons for the increase in road accidents for this age group don't include lack of road safety knowledge. Most pupils can tell you how to cross a road safely. Be sure that pupils' campaigns acknowledge this and don't just focus upon crossing the road safely or cycle safety.

Reasons for an increased chance of being involved in a road traffic accident are:

- Pupils do not know their new route well and might not have worked out the safest places to cross the roads.
- The new journey is often longer.
- In the autumn term, some pupils have to travel home in the dark – especially after the clocks have gone back in October.
- Pupils walking with friends can pay more attention to their peers than the road.
- Pupils might initially worry about being late, therefore rush and take risks.
- Some inexperienced cyclists will be cycling to school for the first time because the journey is a greater distance.
- Pupils may take risks to impress friends.

Share these reasons, then ask pupils to develop a campaign to reduce road accidents for first-year secondary school pupils. Remind them that it is better to address one or two issues really effectively than to try to address them all.

Taking it further

Some of the 'adverts' could be shown in assembly for the rest of the year group or school to see.

Pupils could make posters and/or a TV 'advert' for road safety targeted at this age group. Ask if they can think of anything else to link to their campaign to improve road safety (for example, safest route guidance, high visibility stickers, cycle helmet checks).

New subjects

"Pupils usually encounter new subjects when they get to secondary school and they don't necessarily know what they are at first."

On a typical timetable for first-year secondary school (see Idea 1 – Peek at a week) there will be subjects that pupils don't currently study. This activity helps to clarify what these subjects are.

You will need to adjust this activity depending on the new subjects your pupils will experience. However, this gives you an idea of how to introduce new subjects and explore the activities that will be found in them.

- List all the subjects pupils will have in their first year at secondary school, being sure to include all of the new subjects they will experience. New subjects might include biology, chemistry, physics, a new modern foreign language, philosophy, etc.
- Make a list of example lessons. You could obtain brief descriptions from the secondary schools (this is obviously better), or make up example lessons from the Key Stage 3 curriculum, for example, 'you will learn how copper sulphate reacts to hydrochloric acid'.
- Ask pupils to work in pairs and match each example lesson to the subject they believe it will belong to.
- Go through each lesson, explore pupils' answers and share the correct ones.

This will give pupils a good idea of what each subject is about, and will illustrate that subjects like design and technology can have lots of different components. It will also clarify the difference between biology, physics and chemistry.

Teaching tip

If you do ask the secondary school to provide some brief descriptions of lessons pupils will actually encounter in their first year, ask for exciting examples that show the extent of topics and activities to help enthuse pupils!

Do the lessons change?

"There are usually slightly different expectations about how pupils apply themselves in primary school lessons compared with secondary school lessons."

The amount by which lesson styles change when a pupil goes from primary school to secondary school depends upon the ethos of both schools. Use this activity to help pupils reflect upon potential changes in teaching and learning.

Ask pupils to consider the following ways of teaching and learning and 1) rate them out of ten for how much they enjoy them, and 2) speculate whether there will be more or less of this kind of learning at secondary school. (You might need to clarify what exactly is meant by some of these.)

- Drama
- Poster-making
- Discussion
- Paired work
- Answering written questions
- Filling in missing words on a worksheet
- Note-taking
- Watching a PowerPoint presentation
- Listening to the teacher
- Watching a demonstration
- Topic work – where a topic is covered in several different subjects
- Using a text book
- Independent research (book or internet)
- Writing an essay
- Interpreting diagrams
- Sorting and ordering activities
- Self-assessment
- Watching DVDs
- Problem-solving/puzzles.

Taking it further

You could contact the secondary schools and ask for more information about the teaching and learning methods used most commonly, so that you can give more specific information about this.

Once pupils have considered this list, make them aware that most secondary schools:

- don't teach cross-curricular topics as different lessons are taught by different teachers
- will expect more independent learning than primary schools
- will have many different teachers with many different preferred teaching styles and techniques
- will tend to have more lessons with demonstrations as a greater amount of equipment is used – particularly in sports, science and technology
- expect pupils to do a little more note-taking in lessons
- tend to use more text books in different lessons
- expect pupils to use the internet as a resource for homework
- will get pupils to self-assess and peer-assess more often
- tend to make all lessons the same length of time, so lessons that might have been short at primary school (for example, French or drama) will go on for longer at secondary school.

Bonus idea

Ask pupils to vote on the method of learning they like least, and then explore what it is about this method that pupils perceive they will (or actually) struggle with. Go on to provide some advice about this method and tips about how to get better at it, or even have a go at practising it!

On time

"Being on time holds more significance to some people than others. Generally those who don't regard being on time as important, tend to be late!"

Because pupils are more likely to be travelling independently, usually for greater distances, and because there is slightly more organisation required at secondary school, some pupils can be prone to lateness. Explore the importance of being on time for school and how to ensure it.

Some people are more likely to be late than others. This is because some people are more prone to distraction and have less awareness of time than others. Explore this idea with pupils by asking:

- Do you often arrive late to things you have been invited to?

or

- When you have been invited somewhere, do you make sure you arrive on time?

Explain that getting to school on time is important. Ask pupils to write a list of things that they think could make someone late for school (for example, alarm not set early enough, having to search for something just before you leave, getting distracted by friends).

From the list they have written, ask pupils to write their top tips for getting to school on time. For example:

- Set your alarm to make sure you allow plenty of time to get ready in the morning.
- Pack your school bag the night before to prevent you from having to search around for things in the morning.
- Don't stand around talking to friends on the street. Remember to keep travelling!

Taking it further

Ask pupils how much they currently rely upon the adults at home to get to school on time. For example: 'Do your parents/carers wake you up? Do they remind you what to take to school or pack your bag for you? Do they make sure you have left by a certain time? Do they keep you on track with your morning routine?' Ask what they could do that would mean they relied on their parents/carers less.

Making new friends

"Some pupils have no difficulty making new friends, others find it really difficult – and the rest are in-between the two!"

There will still be a lot of new faces at secondary school, and while being friendly and connecting with others comes easily to some, others find it quite daunting. Develop some advice about making new friends.

Ask pupils to work with a partner to discuss the following.

- Imagine walking into a room full of strangers. How would this make you feel, and what would you do?
- How would you feel if you found out that everyone in that room was a stranger to everyone else: better or worse?
- If nobody was speaking to anyone, what could you say to start up a conversation?
- If suddenly you saw someone you knew, what would you do?

Explain that this is a little like arriving at secondary school on the first day. What advice can pupils give themselves to help them make friends. You could incorporate the following advice.

- Try to start up conversations instead of waiting for others to come to you. If everyone waited, nothing would happen.
- Make the effort to talk to people you don't know – they will appreciate your friendliness.
- Give everyone a chance. Don't judge people by what they look like.
- Remember nobody gets on with everyone. It will take time to find really good friends.
- Treat others as you would like to be treated. Think about what this really means.

Taking it further

Ask pupils to make a list of 'things friendly people do', such as: asking questions and showing an interest, listening attentively, giving compliments, joining in and asking others if they would like to join in, offering help, making eye contact and smiling, laughing at people's jokes. You could also ask them to list behaviours that would seem unfriendly.

First impressions

"We rarely wonder what first impression we make as we usually just get on and be ourselves – as we should. Unfortunately, however, people tend to judge us within the very first few seconds of meeting us – so first impressions do often count".

Approaching and talking to people we don't yet know can be an intimidating task – even for seemingly confident people. Ask pupils to consider good things to say to a stranger to start up a conversation and make a good first impression.

Teaching tip

This activity links well with Idea 40 – Making new friends.

Ask pupils to work in pairs to create and act out two scenarios: 1) the world's worst first encounter, and 2) the world's best first encounter. Allow them time to develop their ideas, then ask some volunteers to demonstrate their drama.

Ask pupils to make two lists during the dramas: 1) things that make a good first encounter, and 2) things that make a bad first encounter! Discuss the lists at the end.

Ask pupils which of the following might be good to say to someone they did not know, on their first day at secondary school.

- Which primary school did you go to?
- I am brilliant at everything. I will be in the top sets for sure.
- Did you look forward to coming here?
- I have an older brother at this school already so I know everything about it.
- Do you live near this school?
- My primary school was the best of all the ones around here.
- I felt a little bit nervous about coming here. Did you?

Taking it further

Use the internet to investigate 'good rapport' and share your findings with your pupils. Gaining good rapport is a skill that comes naturally to most people but, for those for whom it doesn't, it is a skill that can be learnt.

Explain that people are more comfortable with someone who shows an interest in them than with someone who boasts or just talks about themselves.

Anti-bullying

Part 4

Define bullying

"It's a good idea to revisit anti-bullying before pupils head off to secondary school, and a good place to start is to define what bullying is."

It is important that pupils have a clear definition of bullying so they know when help is needed — for themselves or for others. Use this activity to fine-tune understanding of what bullying is and is not.

Taking it further

Ask pupils to work in pairs to write a definition of bullying. Helpful sentence starters are: 'A person is being bullied if . . .' or 'Bullying is when . . .'.

Bonus idea ★

Find a selection of definitions for bullying from the internet and ask pupils which one they prefer. Ask pupils to split the definitions up into the three components: 1) done deliberately, 2) done over a period of time, and 3) there is a power imbalance.

Read these statements aloud one at a time and ask pupils to categorise each one as 'bullying' (B), 'not bullying' (NB) or 'can't tell' (CT).

- Sam told Ashley that her work was rubbish. (CT)
- Gina accidentally tripped Mo up. (NB)
- Every morning Lubna teased Caroline on her way to school. (Probably B, but can't tell completely because it might be well intentioned and not bother Caroline.)
- Ben pushed Marley in the playground. (CT)
- Every break time Clara made Anu hand over some of her dinner money so Anu had less lunch than she used to have. Anu hated this happening but did not know what to do about it. (B)
- Every time Dan played football, Gary and his mates laughed and said he was rubbish. Dan was always upset. (B)
- Tom got cross and snapped at Frankie because he nudged him and made him make a mistake with his painting. (NB)

Hopefully this will clarify that bullying has three components:

1 The nasty act is done deliberately.
2 It is nearly always done repeatedly.
3 The target feels unable to stick up for themselves.

Smash the bullying stereotype

"There is always an assumption that the big kid bullies the little kid. This is certainly not always the case and everyone needs to know this."

Sometimes, a situation is not seen as bullying because it does not conform to the stereotype of a bigger, stronger boy bullying a weaker one. Help pupils develop a deeper understanding of what bullying is by exploring and challenging some stereotypes of bullies and victims.

Give pupils a sheet of paper divided in two. Ask them to draw a bully on one side and the person they have been bullying on the other side. Ask pupils to make up and label the following details for both the bully and the person being bullied:

- name
- age
- family background
- interests
- house
- the way s/he speaks
- the ways/he behaves at school.

Explore the characters that pupils have developed. Chances are the bully will be large and thuggish, and the person being bullied will be younger and smaller. Challenge these stereotypes. In reality, bullies and victims can be nothing like we expect; it is important to be aware of this.

Explain that bullying has included situations in the past where younger children have bullied older children, girls have bullied boys, pupils who do well at school have bullied other pupils who do well, etc. Emphasise the definition of bullying (see Idea 42 – Define bullying) and stress that if the three factors of bullying are present, then it is bullying – whoever is involved.

Taking it further

Discuss why a boy being bullied by a girl or a large pupil being bullied by a smaller pupil might be less likely to report the bullying and seek help. Stress the part of the bullying definition that says that if the target of the bullying feels like they cannot do anything to prevent it, then it is bullying and they need to find some help.

Forms of bullying

"Since social media has become such a significant part of the vast majority of young people's lives, bullying has so many more platforms for working its damage."

Learning about the different types of bullying can help pupils to recognise it is happening the moment it starts, and make its chances of being reported more likely. Take time to explore the variety of ways that one person can bully another.

Teaching tip

While it is really important to raise anti-bullying awareness, it is also important to keep its likelihood of happening in perspective. Take some time to explain to pupils that many people make it through their school life without ever being bullied.

Revisit the definition of bullying: bullying is where somebody is deliberately nasty to another person more than once (usually over a period of time) in a way that the person being bullied does not feel like they can defend themselves.

Ask pupils to work in groups and list all the ways a person could be bullied with this definition in mind.

If pupils struggle, give them the following clues:

- Bullying is not just about hitting.
- A person can bully from a distance.
- Bullying can be about what you don't do as much as what you do actually do.
- Bullies sometimes pick on differences.
- Some of the worst bullying just uses words – and these are sometimes written.
- Finding ways of embarrassing another person can be bullying.

Once pupils feel their lists are complete, go through a comprehensive list of ways people can bully and ask if they missed any of them.

Reiterate that bullying always needs to be reported.

Cyberbullying

"The speed at which an image or piece of information can be spread around the internet, and the fact it can happen at any time of the day or night, makes cyberbullying potentially extremely harmful."

Cyberbullying – using technology to pass on information, images or messages that upset another person – is a particularly potent form of bullying. As pupils head towards the teenage years and gain access to more technology, the chance of cyberbullying increases. Raise awareness of this issue and of how pupils can protect themselves.

- Never share a picture or piece of information that you would not be happy for absolutely anyone to see. A friend might wrongly assume it's OK to share, then accidental cyberbullying will happen as others pass the picture on.
- Never reply or retaliate if someone uses technology to be nasty to you as this will probably make it worse.
- Always report cyberbullying. If the first adult you report it to doesn't help, keep reporting it to adults you trust until someone does help.
- Keep all evidence (emails, email addresses and any messages that offend) – never delete them. This will make it much easier to tackle cyberbullying.
- On many websites, you can block messages from individuals if you report that they have been cyberbullying you. Mobile phone companies can also block certain phone numbers.
- Schools have a responsibility to deal with any bullying that is reported to them, even if it happens out of school hours. If you are bullied in any way, including cyberbullying, tell a member of staff.

Teaching tip

After sharing this advice with pupils, check that they understand by asking them to write down three key pieces of information that they remember.

Taking it further

Many anti-bullying websites offer further advice about how to tackle cyberbullying (alongside pieces of advice about bullying generally). Make pupils aware of these websites, for example: www.bullying.co.uk/cyberbullying; www.childline.org.uk; www.nspcc.org.uk.

What to do about bullying?

"It's no good just being able to recognise bullying – you've got to know what to do about it when it happens."

Just as important as developing understanding about bullying is the knowledge of what to do about it when it happens. Develop the understanding in your pupils that we all have the right not to be bullied and that we might sometimes need to persist a little in finding help that is effective enough to stop the bullying.

Give pupils the following information:

- If you think you are being bullied or you witness someone else being bullied, you need to report this to an adult.
- If nothing happens to stop the bullying, you need to find another adult to tell.
- You need to keep telling until something happens to make the bullying stop.

Ask pupils, in small groups, to develop a school campaign that will get this message across to every pupil in the school. Ask:

- How and when will you get this message to everyone? Will you use more than one method?
- What will be the name of your campaign? (Understand bullying, Act now – no to bullying)
- What words and/or pictures will you use to get the message across?
- Will your campaign have a logo?
- How will you check that every child has received and understood the message? (Spot checks, bullying quizzes, ask parents/carers to ask their children.)

Ask each group of pupils to present their ideas to the rest of the class. Get the class to vote on which campaign they think will work the best. The whole class could then support the delivery of this campaign.

Taking it further

Schools that tackle bullying effectively develop a 'culture of telling'. This means that every pupil – whether they are being bullied or they witness someone else being bullied – knows they need to tell an adult they trust, and they usually know who to tell. You could add this element to their campaign. In other words, how would they create a culture of telling within the school?

Child-speak

"Working with pupils to create child-friendly policies is always worthwhile."

Involving pupils in developing a child-friendly anti-bullying policy is a brilliant way of raising anti-bullying awareness.

Explain to pupils what a policy is. (A set of procedures and guidelines, written down to explain how everyone in a school will do a certain task or approach a particular issue.) Give an example like: a school's marking policy will tell all the teachers in the school how to mark their books and what system to use.

Explain that pupils' help is needed to write an anti-bullying policy. Give groups of pupils a sheet of A3 paper with the following questions scattered over the sheet.

- What is bullying?
- What are the different forms of bullying?
- How will pupils be encouraged to report bullying?
- Who can pupils report bullying to?
- What will happen to make sure everyone (adults and children) understands what bullying is and what to do about it?
- What will happen when bullying is reported?
- How will the adults in school make sure the bullying has stopped?
- How will parents/carers be involved when bullying happens?
- Who in schools will keep a record of any bullying and how will they do it?

Ask pupils to discuss each question and jot down their ideas to answer these questions. Next, collate the ideas as a class to produce a pupil-friendly anti-bullying policy.

Taking it further

Pupils could develop a bullying questionnaire to investigate younger pupils' understanding of bullying and/or a questionnaire to investigate any pupil's experience of bullying.

Bonus idea ★

Ask pupils to produce an even simpler illustrated policy or leaflet aimed at young children.

Anti-bullying quiz

"A true or false quiz is a really quick and effective way of 'revising' anti-bullying."

It's important to revisit the issue of anti-bullying. Many schools do this every year during Anti-Bullying Week in November. As a minimum, you need to check that everyone still understands what bullying is and what they need to do about it if it happens. Turning this into a quiz really engages pupils and gets them thinking about the issues surrounding bullying.

Involving parents

Pupils could either take this quiz home or produce one of their own and take it home for parents to complete with the aim of prompting some discussion between parents/carers and their children about anti-bullying. This will help raise awareness of this important issue with the adults at home.

Create a true or false anti-bullying quiz that includes the key issues about bullying that you need pupils to be aware of. Here are some example statements:

- Only boys bully. (False)
- Bullying can cause a lot of suffering and make people really miserable. It can make them really ill and not want to come to school. (True)
- Only weak people get bullied. (False)
- Bullying should always be reported to an adult. (True)
- Schools have to know what they are going to do when bullying has been reported. (True)
- If you see someone being bullied, the best thing to do is report it to an adult straightaway. (True)
- Some people deserve to be bullied. (False)
- If someone says something nasty to you once, you are definitely being bullied. (False)
- A bully is deliberately nasty to someone – usually several times. (True)
- If you tell an adult that you are being bullied and nothing happens, you need to tell another adult. (True)
- Some bullies use the internet or mobile phones to bully people. It's never a good idea to give your phone number out to everyone. (True)

- If you see someone being bullied, you should go and tell an adult as soon as you can. (True)
- Bullies are always bigger than the people they bully. (False)
- Spreading nasty rumours or deliberately leaving someone out can be bullying. (True)
- If someone is being picked on again and again and they feel like they cannot stick up for themselves, this is bullying. (True)
- If you witness bullying you should help to defend the person being bullied. (False – unless you are sure you will not get hurt yourself, it is better to go and find help.)
- Some adults don't understand how serious bullying is. (True)
- Bullying always involves violence. (False).
- ChildLine (0800 1111) is a number you can ring for free to help if you are being bullied. (True)
- Bullying can happen to anyone. (True)

Bonus idea

A quiz like this could be part of an anti-bullying class assembly – with pretend contestants answering. Also included in the assembly could be:

- a clear definition of bullying

- information telling you what to do if you are bullied

- freeze-frames to illustrate the different types of bullying – with someone interviewing the 'frozen' people

- a short play that demonstrates the suffering bullying can cause.

ChildLine

"ChildLine is a fantastic resource for children and young people. It is important that we let them know about it and what it can do for them."

Some pupils have no problem articulating their worries and concerns, but others have real trouble. Some pupils have adults at home that listen attentively to them, others don't. Tell pupils about ChildLine — if it means that just one child has access to an extra line of support, then it will be worth it!

Teaching tip

It's easy to assume that every child knows about ChildLine, but make doubly sure they do by making reference to it regularly in PSHE lessons. Give some examples of the kinds of problems children ring ChildLine with to illustrate the scope: puberty, bullying, getting used to a new step-parent, problems with brothers or sisters, homework.

- Request posters from www.childline.org.uk and display them in every classroom.
- Mention ChildLine regularly in assemblies.
- Include the ChildLine number and a brief description of what it does on newsletters that go home.

ChildLine has trained counsellors that will listen to children and young people about any problem — however big or small it seems. Their counsellors are not easily shocked and they have spoken to children with many different problems. They have had so many calls, it is unlikely that a problem will be new to them. Also make pupils aware that ChildLine:

- can be rung on 0800 1111
- has other methods of contact, including email and online chat
- is confidential — they will only say or do something if you ask them to, or if there is a risk of serious harm
- is free, and will not appear on the phone bill
- can be rung 24 hours a day
- has a website with lots of advice and support for children and young people.

Being yourself

Part 5

Decisions decisions

"Part of growing up is that you get more choices and therefore get to make more decisions!"

Making a choice can be very hard, and working out what the best choice is can pose terrible dilemmas. As pupils grow up, it is inevitable that they will have more choices and more decisions to make. Spend a PSHE lesson or two looking at decisions and how to make them!

There are several activities you can do to explore decisions and how to make them. Here are some to start you off.

1 Explore the reasons behind making decisions. Give pupils the selection of reasons below and ask them to make up something that a person could have decided to do for each reason. Next, ask pupils to sort the reasons into good and bad motives for making each decision. This usually stimulates lots of discussion.

- Because we enjoy it.
- Because it is the easiest thing to do.
- Because someone has pressurised us.
- Because we fancy a change.
- Because everyone else is doing it.
- Because we think it will make us look good in others' eyes.
- Because it makes life easier or better in some way.
- To try and make someone like us.
- Because it creates opportunities for us and makes life more interesting.
- To protect ourselves from harm.
- To get out of doing something else.
- Because we think it will make us feel better.
- Because it is habit.

2 Ask pupils to imagine that a person has a big decision to make (for example, whether or not to change jobs, whether or not to join a sports team) and they don't know which choice to take. Ask pupils to work in groups to create a list of advice about making decisions. Pupils could use the internet to investigate this. The advice might include:

- Never make a decision when you are emotionally charged. Wait until you are calm.
- Find out as much information as you can about the choices available.
- Make sure you know all the choices available. Is there a compromise?
- Get feedback and advice from others.
- Sleep on it! Quite often when we can't decide, we can wake up feeling certain about which choice to take.
- Imagine you had made one choice. How does it make you feel/think? Then imagine you had made the other choice.
- Write down the pros and cons of each choice. Mark each one out of ten for how significant it is.
- Listen to your gut – what is it telling you to do?

3 Give pupils some dilemmas to explore. For example:

- You are in the park with a load of mates. One of them offers you a cigarette and teases you for not trying it. What do you do?
- You find a £10 note in the cloakroom at school. What do you do?
- You are with a group of children in the playground and they all start saying unkind things about one of your mates. What do you do?

Explain that when we have a really difficult dilemma there is part of us that wants one thing and another part that wants something else. For each dilemma above, what are the two parts? How can knowing the parts help us make a good decision?

Taking it further

Explore the idea that some decisions we make will cause changes. Some people have stronger negative emotional reactions to change than others. Ask pupils to think about a decision they made that caused a change. How did they feel about this change? Do they think they are someone who is more likely to make choices that mean things stay the same or not?

Bonus idea ★

Ask pupils to keep a decision diary. They should list any choices they were faced within a week and how they made their decisions. You could also ask them to rate how difficult the decision was to make (0 being very easy and 10 being really difficult).

Rights and responsibilities

"Being all 'rights' without 'responsibilities' is not healthy or realistic!"

Getting more freedom and wishing to make more decisions for yourself is a normal part of growing up. This simple activity helps pupils understand that increased rights and freedom cause the need for increased responsibility.

Ask what is meant by 'rights' and 'responsibilities.' Ask pupils to define both.

Explain that as pupils get older they will want more freedom and to be able to make more decisions for themselves. Ask pupils to work in pairs and make a list of what they would like more freedom with as they get older. Give the example that they might want to be able to choose when they complete their homework (rather than being told when to do it).

Explain that with every expectation of more freedom, they will be trusted to make responsible choices. For example, if they want to be able to choose when to complete their homework, they will have the responsibility of making sure they complete it in time.

Ask pupils to work through their list of expected freedoms and list the corresponding responsibilities. For example:

Taking it further

Explore the idea that negotiations with parents/carers for extra freedom will always go better if a pupil demonstrates that they will behave responsibly!

- Freedom: Be able to go to a town or city with friends. Responsibilities: To behave sensibly, to be home when they are expected, to be contactable by mobile phone, to make careful arrangements to meet friends.
- Freedom: To have a mobile phone. Responsibilities: To look after it and ensure it does not get lost or damaged.

Who is there?

"It is important to make kids aware that there is support out there if they need it."

Helping pupils to clarify a support network not only highlights the fact everyone needs help now and then, but also means that they are more likely to access it if they need to.

To consider support networks, start by asking pupils to think about which friend they would turn to if:

- they needed to borrow a pencil
- they felt a bit sad and needed cheering up
- they had something to tell but wanted it kept secret
- they wanted an idea for what to buy someone for their birthday
- they had a crush on someone and it was not making them feel good
- they had not heard what the teacher said in a lesson.

Next explain that some problems cannot be sorted by talking to a friend (for example, bullying, homework troubles, feeling ill) and therefore usually need an adult to help. Ask pupils to identify and list five adults they trust: five adults they would be happy to turn to if they needed help with something. These adults could include a parent/carer, a neighbour, a relative, a teacher, a teaching assistant, a midday supervisor, a friend of the family, club leaders, a school nurse, or a doctor.

Stress that if pupils do not get the help they need from one adult, they need to keep finding adults to talk to until they do get the right help.

Teaching tip

As children grow up, they tend to move away from being dependent upon their parents/carers. Perhaps suggest that pupils only include one parent/carer in their list to ensure there are four other adults outside the immediate family that they would be happy to seek help from.

Taking it further

Ask pupils to think of the person that they think would be most supportive and useful for sharing any worries with about moving up to secondary school.

Bonus idea ★

Pupils could draw their support network in a pictorial metaphor, for example, writing names on the fingers of a helping hand, on the roots of a tree, on a signpost, on the petals of a flower, etc.

Help!

"Some people see asking for help as a weakness. Not being able to ask for help is a weakness in my opinion."

Knowing when to seek help is a life skill. Spend time making pupils aware of the signs and circumstances that indicate it is time to find some assistance and support from an adult.

Taking it further

Ask pupils to create an advert that sells the idea that asking for help is a clever thing to do to really drive home this message.

Explain the following to pupils:

- It is normal in our lives to feel a range of emotions – some that feel good and some not so good. However, if anyone feels low and miserable for a very long time, chances are they need some help.
- If you are losing sleep because of something that is happening or a worry you are having, you need to get an adult to help.
- Some problems are very difficult for a child or young person to sort out on their own.
- If something is worrying you so that it is all that you are thinking about, you need to find an adult to talk to.

Ask pupils to compose a list of situations and worries that they think a pupil should get help from an adult with. For example:

- being bullied
- struggling with school work
- worries about puberty
- an adult touching you or behaving in a way that made you uncomfortable
- someone trying to persuade you to do something that might cause harm
- becoming ill
- being unhappy about arguments that are happening at home.

Explain that not every adult is good at helping. That is why it is a good idea to have a few adults in mind that you could turn to.

Bonus idea ★

Ask pupils to discuss why some people find it hard to ask for help. Explore what it might be that makes a person scared to ask for help.

E-safety

"We can't possibly watch over our children all the time or censor what they are exposed to."

As pupils get older, they will use computers more, for both research and social networking. Visiting (or revisiting) e-safety guidelines before secondary school is time well spent.

Make e-safety guidance cards and hand them out to small groups of children. Ask each group to discuss the reason for the advice. Then ask each group to read out their advice and give the reason for it.

- Only give your email address and mobile number to friends you completely trust.
- Never pass on someone's email address or phone number without permission.
- Always keep your phone with you, or somewhere that nobody else can get it.
- Don't use your real name on social networking sites. (Many people do not follow this piece of advice.)
- Never post personal details (for example, address, school name, family details or phone numbers) on a social networking site.
- Never tell anyone your passwords.
- Never reply to nasty messages – save them and show them to an adult.
- Think carefully before posting a photo or video online, and never post one of a friend without their permission.
- Never feel pressurised to post a photo or send a message by phone.
- Never arrange to meet someone you only know through the internet.
- Block any website with information or images that upset you.
- Block anyone who makes you very uncomfortable or upset with what they have written on a social network site.

Teaching tip

Explain that there are some dangerous adults who set out to trick children and young people into seeing them using the internet. Also explain that another problem with the internet and mobile phones is that once a picture has been posted it can travel to a very large number of people very quickly.

Dangers and risks

"With greater freedom, less supervision, quick communication via email, a need to rebel, push boundaries and risk-take and, for some, a sometimes less than sensible peer influence, secondary pupils have a greater chance of encountering dangers."

Not every secondary school pupil will engage in risk-taking behaviours, but there is an increased likelihood of them doing so in their teenage years compared to their childhood. Spend time exploring the issue of risk-taking and the possible reasons for it.

Explain to pupils that:

- Every generation of teenagers has wanted to push the boundaries.
- Testing and pushing boundaries is a natural part of growing up.
- The teenage brain is wired up to take more risks than its pre-teen self.
- Some teenagers harm themselves because of their need to test the limits.
- Peer influence, or doing something to impress friends, can encourage teenagers to take risks.
- Photos of dangerous actions are sometimes posted on social networking sites and often get 'liked' by friends. This encourages risk-taking behaviour.

Guide a discussion about risk-taking behaviours using the following questions.

1 What kind of risks do you think some teenagers take? (Not keeping safe on the roads, drinking alcohol, doing dares.)
2 Why do you think some teenagers do this? (To impress, to get a thrill, to rebel.)
3 Some teenagers push themselves really hard, but in healthy ways. What 'healthy' ways can you think of? (Becoming superfit, pursuing exciting sports.)

Risk reduction, not elimination

"Effective health and safety education acknowledges all possibilities and their related risks."

Consider how you deliver drug education. Do you simply tell pupils not to smoke and explain how it is bad for you, or do you acknowledge the fact that some people smoke and explore the reasons why some people make this choice and others don't and consider the impact of both choices? Review how you deliver health education and set out to make it more effective for pupils about to go to secondary school.

Most people, particularly teenagers, don't like being told not to do something. Simply telling someone not to smoke, have underage sex or drink alcohol is unlikely to work. A more effective approach:

- acknowledges all the choices and that some people take each of them
- considers the pros and cons of all choices
- does not tell anyone what to do or not to do
- does not judge one choice to be superior to another
- does not lead pupils to develop an exaggerated idea of how many people are taking part in a particular activity
- equips pupils to make their own choices based on all the information
- explores the reasons behind certain health choices
- does not use shock tactics to try and prevent certain behaviours, as these can present unrealistic or extreme images that pupils cannot relate to.

Consider if, and how this approach would alter some of your PSHE lessons to more effectively promote healthy choices.

> **Teaching tip**
>
> Reasons why people make non-healthy choices include: peer pressure, peer influence (to impress friends), they have developed a hard habit to break, exploration, to rebel, a temporary nice sensation, lack of self-respect or self-esteem.

StereoTYPICAL

"Grumpy, moody, totally misunderstood and alien to their parents – are teenagers really like this?"

Explore the emotional and social changes pupils are likely to experience in the early days of secondary school by exploring the stereotype of a teenager.

Pupils are likely to have heard references to young people being 'very teenage' – especially if they have older siblings. Ask pupils to draw a stereotypical teenager and label him or her with the typical emotional and behavioural attributes of a teenager.

Pupils might say that they slam doors, have mood swings, are self-conscious, shout at parents, want to impress their friends. Ask if the following facts explain the stereotype.

- The teenage years are a transition from being a child to being an adult.
- Some people find the teenage years really difficult, others less so.
- Teenagers usually want more freedom than they had as a child. This is part of growing up but it can cause conflicts with parents/carers.
- The hormones that cause puberty can make teenagers moody and sensitive.
- Sometimes when a parent/carer says something like, 'Have you packed your bag?' a teenager hears, 'I don't trust you to do anything.'
- There are huge changes going on in the teenage brain. This can make them disorganised and clumsy.
- Teenagers start to grow away from their parents/carers and their friends become more important to them.

Painfully self-conscious

"It is a mixture of awkwardness, embarrassment and feeling like everyone is looking at you – and not in a kind way."

An increase in self-consciousness tends to start at the top end of primary school and continues through much of secondary school. It can cause incredible discomfort and distress. Use these ideas to help pupils consider and develop strategies for dealing with self-consciousness.

Ask pupils to write a sentence that explains what self-consciousness feels like.

Ask pupils which of the following would make them feel self-conscious:

- falling off a bike in a busy street
- walking into a silent class late
- standing up in assembly
- reading aloud in class
- being told that your top is on inside out
- being told off in front of your friends.

Ask small groups of pupils to develop advice to cope with feeling self-conscious, such as:

- Most of the time, only you will notice the thing that makes you feel self-conscious.
- Smile, laugh at yourself and pretend you are not feeling self-conscious. This helps!
- Everyone feels self-conscious sometimes. If you are kind to others when they feel it, they are more likely to be kind to you.
- People will soon forget what happened.
- If someone laughs at you, tell them directly that 'that is really unkind'.
- Take a deep breath and tell yourself that 'it will be OK' over and over again.
- Imagine nobody is paying any attention.

If possible, share a personal anecdote of something that made you feel self-conscious to show that it can happen to anyone.

Taking it further

The changes of puberty can make children feel extra self-conscious. Remind pupils that everyone goes through it and that it is unkind to comment negatively on anyone else's' appearance.

Bonus idea

Ask pupils to imagine that they have just realised that a friend is feeling self-conscious because they had their flies undone/ skirt tucked into their knickers/fallen over. What would be the best response for making this friend feel better?

Puberty

"Pupils are coping with an awful lot of change in a relatively short period of time."

Use this checklist to ensure that all relevant aspects of puberty have been covered before your pupils leave primary school.

Teaching tip

You can obtain free leaflets from the NHS or other organisations that give children information about the changes that happen at puberty.

- Physical changes in puberty, and the practicalities of dealing with periods and wet dreams.
- The emotional aspects of puberty.
- The names for external sexual organs.
- Puberty can start anywhere between the ages of 8 and 14. It can feel awkward to be the first or the last to start.
- Puberty brings a lot of change in a short time, but everyone goes through it. It helps to talk to someone to about the changes being experienced. Most changes take a while to get used to.
- You might feel self-conscious during puberty, but you are likely to be the only person that has noticed whatever it is that is making you feel this way.
- It is totally inappropriate to make fun of, or personal comments about, any changes that happen during puberty.
- Many young people wonder if they are 'normal' during puberty. This can be part of adapting to a changing body.
- Hormones can make you feel happy one minute and grumpy or tearful the next. They do eventually settle down.
- During puberty, young people often start to fancy other people. This can cause distress, worry or very intense feelings. It is a good idea to talk concerns through with a trusted friend or adult.
- Start paying more attention to personal hygiene at the onset of puberty.

Involving parents

It is a great idea to set 'homework' to encourage discussions between parents/carers and their children about the changes of puberty. This could simply include a male and a female outline on a sheet with the instructions that pupils get their parents/carers to help them label all the changes that happen.

Hormones!

"A really significant part of puberty is the impact hormones have on a young person."

Hormones are the chemical messengers in the body that trigger the changes of puberty, but they have some side effects too. Make pupils aware of their impact and provide advice for dealing with them.

Hormones are powerful things and teenagers are often described as having rampaging hormones! This is because their bodies are undergoing significant physical changes driven by hormones – which also have some side effects (see online resources). Ask pupils to sort a list of side effects into those that can happen at puberty and those that don't.

Dealing with these side effects is easier said than done. Ask pupils to think what advice they could give to someone who is experiencing them, such as:

- Remember, puberty does not last forever.
- Remember, friends are going through this too – talk to them about difficulties.
- Keep a diary and write down all the things on your mind – it can help.
- If you get extreme acne, visit a doctor.
- Be kind to yourself! Don't be cross with yourself when you make mistakes.
- Get plenty of rest, eat well, exercise and look after your personal hygiene.
- Take time out from social networking, as it can be emotionally intense.
- Take deep breaths, go for a walk, have some quiet times where you just read a book or do an activity you really like.
- Tell people how you are feeling.

> **Bonus idea** ★
>
> Get pupils to make personal 'when it all gets too much' posters, full of suggestions and advice, to advise their future selves.

Changing tastes

"You will still be you, but you will start to like doing different things."

Reflecting upon how interests change as children and young people get older, illustrates that interests will inevitably change and that this is a healthy part of growing up.

Get each pupil to create a personal timeline that includes their life so far but that also projects up to the age of 18. Ask pupils to label the timeline so far with major events in their lives (for example, moving house, getting a baby brother or sister, memorable holidays, etc.). Then ask pupils to add pictures of things they liked to do at different ages. This can include:

- toys and games they enjoyed
- activities they did outside
- TV programmes they liked to watch
- computer or game console activities
- activities they did with their parents/carers
- places they liked to go to
- activities they did that meant they got exercise
- food they liked to eat
- what they enjoyed at school
- what they did with friends.

Next, ask pupils to project into the future by adding activities to their timeline that they think they will enjoy doing at different ages. Pupils can use the headings above to help. Ask pupils to share their timeline with a friend and discuss:

- What do you think you will always like doing?
- Why have you included what you have on your future timeline?

Healthy habits

"It's easy to forget to look after your health when you are a teenager."

Delivering a generic health promotion session that explores the difficulties some people have when making healthy choices, before pupils leave for secondary school, is time well spent.

Give the following list of subtitles:

- eating food high in sugar, salt and fat
- sleep
- eating fruit and vegetables
- stress
- smoking
- drinking alcohol
- drinking water
- exercise
- dental hygiene.

Ask pupils to write a sentence for each subtitle that explains the healthy choice for each one. Then, discuss as a class the question 'If we know what the healthy choices are, what stops everyone from just getting on and doing them?'

Ask why some teenagers find it hard to make healthy choices, and discuss the reasons.

Ask pupils which healthy options they personally find the hardest to take. Discuss the fact that it is sometimes hard to see the benefits of choosing the healthy options. However, young people who do make healthy choices tend to:

- have better concentration
- sleep well
- have more energy
- be much less likely to feel depressed
- have clearer skin
- be ill less often.

Taking it further

Ask pupils to set themselves three health challenges to try and keep over the next four weeks. Ask pupils how they will record how well they do with these challenges, or monitor everyone's progress as a class.

Bonus idea ★

Ask pupils to create posters that specifically aim to persuade teenagers to make healthy choices. (Pupils can focus on one health issue or try to include them all.)

Who am I?

"You spend the first part of your life developing who you are."

Once you have self-awareness, you can get on with developing self-acceptance. Helping pupils to understand their preferences, values and prevalent personality traits can help them find their passions and, on a more practical level, aim for appropriate careers!

Involving parents

Send pupils home with a list of positive personality traits and ask parents/carers to mark out of ten how much they think their child has each quality. This will spark discussions about personality.

There are many different ways of exploring personalities. Here are a few to start you off.

1 Exploring preferences and what they tell you about yourself: give pupils a list of 'would you rather . . .' choices (see the online resources for examples) and ask them to indicate which they would prefer. Once complete, ask pupils to work in pairs to see what their preferences tell them about themselves. Ask pupils to write down any information they gather about themselves.

2 Lists of traits: ask pupils to mark themselves out of ten for how much a selection of personality traits (see the online resources for example traits) could be used to describe them.

3 Spectrums: in a large space create the following imaginary spectrums and ask pupils to stand in the position that reflects how much or little of each of the following traits they think they have.

- The worry spectrum. Some people worry more than others. Position yourself on the spectrum to indicate how much you think you worry compared with others.
- The introvert/extrovert spectrum. Some people are outgoing, happy to mix with lots of people and share their thoughts readily. Others are happy with their own company, thinking things through by themselves.

- The imagination/practical spectrum. Some people like to be hands on, practical and down to earth. Others prefer to use their imagination, can see how to do things without actually doing them and often think about the future.
- The planning/flexibility spectrum. Some people like to be organised, make plans and stick to them. Others are more spontaneous, flexible and change their minds a lot.
- The feeling/thinking spectrum. Some people make decisions based on a gut reaction and how the decision will affect other people, others apply logic to find the decision that just makes most sense.

4 Values: ask pupils to put the following values in a hierarchy from those that are most important to them to those that are least important:

- being healthy
- being able to forgive people
- being generous
- being sensible
- being adventurous
- being good-looking
- being different and standing out from the crowd
- being interesting
- having lots of friends
- being famous
- being fit and sporty
- being rich
- being kind to others
- being happy
- never being bored
- being grateful.

Taking it further

When pupils have a list of strengths, preferences and qualities, ask them to think about a job that would use some of these.

Bonus idea ★

There are many free online personality profiling tests. Search the internet for Myers-Briggs, the Big Five or Enneagram profiling tests. Pupils might wish to take one of these tests at home and see what insights they deliver.

Boost self-esteem

"Sadly self-esteem is not developed overnight for those pupils who need it boosting!"

Every primary school has an ethos to promote and preserve pupils' self-esteem. Helping pupils to develop awareness so they can try and boost their own self-esteem is a very useful tool for pupils as they progress to secondary school. Help pupils reflect upon self-esteem and how they might help themselves develop and maintain a healthy amount.

Start by asking your class what they think self-esteem is. If they struggle, continue by asking which of the following is true about self-esteem and which is false.

- You have good self-esteem if you like yourself. (True)
- Having successes in the things you do helps you develop self-esteem. (True)
- Self-esteem makes people arrogant. (False)
- Self-esteem is about how good we feel about ourselves. (True)
- You cannot develop more self-esteem. (False)
- If you have low self-esteem, you struggle to find things that you like about yourself. (True)
- If you have poor self-esteem, you feel terrible when you make a mistake and this might prevent you from having another go. (True)

Ask pupils how someone with good self-esteem behaves. (They are likely to be confident, not be too upset when they make mistakes, be good at surviving tough times, be willing to have a go at things they know they might find difficult.)

Next, ask pupils to think about a character called John. John has very low self-esteem. Read through the following advice and ask pupils how each piece of advice could help John.

Taking it further

Ask pupils to search the internet for famous sayings that motivate them or make them feel good about themselves. They could illustrate their favourite one and these could be displayed in the classroom.

- Focus on the things you do well. When you have a success, enjoy it.
- When you make a mistake, accept that mistakes happen to everyone and that we can learn from them.
- When someone gives you a compliment, write it down somewhere so you can remember it.
- Remember that nobody gets everything right all of the time.
- Remember that everybody has different strengths.
- Hang out with people who like you and who are kind to you.
- Be determined to think positive thoughts about yourself.
- Make a list of happy times – when you felt good – to read whenever you feel like it.
- Find activities you enjoy and get really good at them. Being an expert or talented at something is really good for your self-esteem.
- Set yourself an aim that is achievable. When you achieve it, be proud of yourself.
- When you think badly of yourself, find evidence that proves it is not true.
- Learn to give people lots of compliments. People who give lots of compliments are more likely to receive them.

Media messages

"Teenagers fall prey to a lot of unhealthy media messages."

The media influences the attitudes our children have about themselves and others. It can have a particularly detrimental effect upon self-image. This is especially unhelpful for pupils about to become very body-conscious as they hit their teenage years. Challenge the idea of what the media would lead us to believe is the only acceptable version of 'attractive'.

Taking it further

Ask pupils to think about how the media makes people behave. What does the media pressurise us to do? What does it make us yearn for? What does it make us think we need? How could it make us feel dissatisfied and always want more or to be different from how we already are? What can it make us feel guilty about? How does it encourage people to get in debt? How might it affect eating habits?

Bonus idea ★

Ask pupils to deliberately deface some adverts. They could have thought bubbles of attractive people having an ordinary thought like, 'Oh no – I forgot to buy some toilet roll,' or they could return the photos to how they were before a computer enhanced them.

Collect plenty of fashion magazines and newspapers with adverts to use in this activity. Give them to the pupils, and ask them to imagine that an alien had received the bundle and has to use them to try and understand what humans are like.

Ask pupils to work in pairs and create a collage poster using the magazines that displays what impression the alien would develop about humans. They should consider what the alien would think about: human skin colour, attractiveness, ability/disability, size, age, hair, skin, financial success, possessions, clothes, how attractive others find you, stress, lifestyle etc.

Ask pupils to present their collages to the class and list the impression the alien would get about humans. Then have a class discussion about the unrealistic impression of humans the alien would receive. Try to cover the following in the discussion:

- How photos in adverts are airbrushed and altered to make legs longer, stomachs flatter, skin clearer, etc.
- How adverts try to sell you a lifestyle and make everything look amazing so that you want to buy their product.
- How very few people look or behave like people in adverts.

Alternative attractiveness guide

"It's very hard to develop a positive self-image when we are bombarded with pictures of attractive people with perfect bodies in the media."

In a world where so much emphasis is placed on looks, many young people develop a poor self-image. Help pupils understand that attractiveness has more to it than just hairstyles, make-up and clothes.

Explain that people can become more attractive, and that you are not talking about make-up, styling hair or choosing the 'right' clothes. Ask whether each item on the following list would make a person seem more attractive, or less:

- showing an interest in others
- scowling and moaning
- being positive and encouraging
- a big smile
- looking confident
- being lazy
- being supportive and willing to help
- being rude
- being lively
- giving compliments
- always putting yourself down
- snapping at people
- holding yourself straight when you walk
- mumbling
- a sense of humour
- being easily persuaded to do things
- slouching
- talking clearly.

Explain that whatever we look like, there are behaviours, ways of holding ourselves and expressions we pull that will make us more or less attractive. Ask pupils to design a magazine page aimed at teenagers entitled, 'the alternative guide to attractiveness'.

Teaching tip

Tell pupils that people become more attractive the more we see them – whatever they look like.

Bonus idea ★

Ask a confident pupil to behave in all the unattractive ways in front of the class, and then do all the attractive things (alternatively, you could demonstrate them). Ask pupils what they thought of the attractive and unattractive behaviours and which person they would most like to meet.

Out and about

"As pupils get older, they get more freedom and this includes freedom to be out and about without adult supervision."

Older pupils will spend more time on their own or with friends in places other than home, especially after starting secondary school. Give them some of these strategies for keeping safe at these times.

- Stay alert. Wearing headphones can make you more prone to road accidents.
- If you are out after dark, stick to busy well-lit streets where possible.
- Always have your mobile phone (if you have one).
- Let your parents/carers know where you are and what time you will get home.
- If you cycle, always wear a helmet and lock up your bike, and never listen to headphones. After dark, wear a high-visibility jacket and use your bike lights.
- Always plan how you will get somewhere and how you will get back.
- Whenever possible, always go places with friends rather than alone.
- Ring home and ask for a lift if you get stuck. Parents/carers would rather come and get you than think you were walking home alone – especially after dark.
- If you get into difficulties when you are out, find a busy place and speak to an adult – preferably someone who is with children, a group of people or a couple.
- If taking a bus alone, sit near the driver.
- If someone tries to take something from you, never fight back – just hand it over.
- Keep valuables out of sight when you are walking around alone.
- If someone stops and asks you for directions, keep your distance from the vehicle while you give them.

Learning how to learn

"There are a variety of ways of learning things. It is important that pupils use strategies that are effective for them."

As pupils venture to secondary school there will be an expectation that they can learn with greater independence. Explore some different ways of learning and investigate which ones pupils think would be most effective for them.

Ask pupils to imagine they are going to learn something new. Then ask them to reflect upon the following questions.

- Do you learn better if you think about what you are learning quietly to yourself or if you have to explain it to someone else?
- Do you learn better if you concentrate for a long time or if you take breaks from concentrating every ten minutes or so?
- Do you learn better if:
  - someone tells you what to do
  - you have pictures to look at that relate to what you are learning
  - you can move around while you learn?
- Do you learn better if you start with the big picture and then learn the details or do you prefer to have the details first?
- Do you learn better in silence or with some background noise?

Ask pupils which of the following they think would help them remember something:

- note-taking
- summarising
- using pictures with labels
- practice questions
- reciting things out loud
- explaining something to someone else
- spider diagrams
- reading about a topic in different places
- acting out what they are learning.

Teaching tip

Share information about how you learnt things best when you had to work independently. What worked well for you and what didn't?

Taking it further

Ask pupils to think of a time when they learnt something really well – something they learnt a while ago but that they can still remember how to do. What happened when they learnt this? Does this give them any clues as to what helps them to learn effectively?

Motivation!

"We can all suffer from lack of motivation – especially when we are having to do a task that we don't want to do!"

With an increase in the amount of independent work secondary school pupils will have to do, there is an increased reliance on pupils being able to motivate themselves. Help pupils find a strategy for getting and staying motivated.

Teaching tip

Demonstrate this method of finding a strategy by talking pupils through an example of your own strategy for getting motivated. This will help pupils understand the process.

Ask pupils to think of a time when they were really motivated to get something done, and they achieved it. It could be anything: learning to skateboard, reading a book, learning how to put up a tent, etc. Ask pupils to write down the thing they were motivated to do.

Now ask pupils to remember the time before they did this thing. What did they tell themselves? What did they say to other people? What did they picture in their head? What did they actually see or look at? What did they feel? What did they do?

Now ask pupils about the time after they had achieved what they set out to do. What did they tell themselves? What did they say to other people? What did they picture in their head? What did they actually see? What did they feel? What did they do?

Pupils should note down the answers to these questions – these are their effective strategies for being motivated. They can use them to get motivated to do anything. If they said to themselves, 'I am going to do this', if they told someone else what they hoped to achieve or they visualised the completed task before they started – then they can use these components of their successful strategy to motivate themselves to do anything!

Bonus idea ★

Find some quotes about motivation on the internet and display them in class.

And relax

"The stresses of everyday life are easier to cope with if we become good at switching off and relaxing."

Adolescence can be a stressful time. Learning methods of relaxation can help young people to cope more effectively with the challenges of teenage life.

Teach pupils what stress is – the hormonal fight or flight response to perceived dangers. This response gears up our bodies for a burst of energy. But this is no good if we don't actually need to fight or run, it can leave us with physical symptoms like a racing heartbeat that can be bad for us in the long run.

Teach pupils that different relaxation techniques exist, for example, yoga and meditation.

Teach pupils a few relaxation techniques, such as:

- Breathing in deeply through the nose and out through the mouth for several minutes. This causes the heart rate to slow down and helps people to feel relaxed.
- Tensing and relaxing different parts of the body. Tense muscles on an in breath and relax them on an out breath.
- Visualise a circle with a dot on its edge. Visualise the dot going round and up on an in breath and round and down on an out breath. Concentrate on making the dot move smoothly.
- Focus on different parts of the body and bit by bit loosen the muscles and relax. Start with the feet, move to the ankles, then the knees, etc.
- Sit quietly and just notice thoughts come into and go out of your head.

Teaching tip

Ask pupils to think of activities that help them to quieten down their mind because they become absorbed in them – activities such as drawing, reading, sport or playing a musical instrument.

Taking it further

Introduce pupils to some relaxation music. Ask how it makes them feel. Explain that relaxing music can be found on video hosting sites on the internet and is another way to become relaxed.

Dealing with emotions

"Emotional literacy makes life much easier to manage and certainly makes the teenage years easier to navigate."

Emotional literacy is being aware of the emotions you are feeling, understanding what might be causing the feeling you are experiencing, knowing the best way to express the feeling, and knowing a good way to respond to other people's feelings. Some people are far more emotionally literate than others. Give pupils a tool to help them develop their emotional literacy further.

As a warm-up, ask pupils to list as many negative emotions as they can think of.

Help pupils to be able to develop their own emotional literacy by giving them the following tool. Explain that this tool can be used by looking back at a time when a negative feeling was experienced.

When you feel an emotion that does not make you feel good:

1 Name the feeling or feelings.
2 Describe the feeling – where in the body do you feel it?
3 Write down the cause or the suspected cause.
4 What did you do as a result of this feeling? Was this a good thing to do?
5 Did what you choose to do affect other people? If so, how?

Ask pupils to work through this process for a recent time when they felt a negative emotion. Explain that the more they use this tool, the more emotionally literate they will become. This will mean they become better and better at dealing with emotions.

Changing relationships

Part 6

Stay in touch

"When you move up to secondary school you can feel a mixture of sadness and excitement. The sadness is mostly about leaving primary school behind."

When pupils finish primary school, encourage them to stay in touch with their close current classmates outside school by creating a friends memory and contact book.

Explain to pupils that friends we make at primary school will always be special. However, when we go to secondary school, we make a lot more friends. Despite this, it is still nice to make contact with our old primary school friends when we need to and to remember happy memories involving them.

To do this, give pupils a home-made contact book, made by folding about six A4 sheets of paper in half. You could also give the booklets a card cover for pupils to decorate. Explain to pupils that they are going to swap their books around with close friends and ask each friend to fill up one of the pages of their book completely.

Each page could include:

- the friend's name
- a small self-portrait of the friend
- the friend's phone number if they are willing to share it
- the friend's email address if they have one (at around this age many children open up an online email account)
- a happy primary school memory or two that the friend shared with you
- a compliment from the friend
- a comment that states what they think and feel about the friendship
- a wish for your future.

Changing relationships

"The move to secondary school and the teenage years bring drastic changes to the relationships you have."

As pupils move to secondary school and head towards their teenage years, the way they relate to the people they know changes. Use this activity to help pupils reflect on this.

Give pupils the following list:

- teachers
- friends
- mum/dad/step-parent/carer
- brothers and sisters
- other relatives
- other adults you know quite well, for example, club leaders.

Ask pupils to list one or two people in each category. Then ask them to use the following questions to compare their relationship with each person when they were aged nine, with how they imagine it will be aged 14.

- How did you spend time together?
- How much time did you spend together each week?
- What did this person do for you?
- How well does this person know you?
- Choose one or two words to describe how you felt about this person.

Discuss as a class how the relationships may have changed, for example:

- Secondary school teachers will know you less well than primary teachers did.
- You will want to spend less time with your family, share less information with them and want more privacy.
- You will spend more time with friends.
- A club leader might become your mentor.

Taking it further

Explore the idea of mentors further (see Idea 94 – Find a mentor). Quite often an adult outside the family, like a music teacher, a sports coach or a neighbour, takes on a guidance role for a young person. This is a healthy way for a young person to access adult support as they start to want to grow away from their family before being fully adult themselves.

Copycats

"As children get older, they care more and more about what their peers think and do."

Peer influence can have a powerful effect on children and teenagers as they fear being picked on for being different or for choices that make them seem 'uncool'. This activity demonstrates the consequences of peer influence so that pupils see how silly it can be.

Peer influence is at its strongest in the first few years of secondary school, and results in someone doing something simply because their peers are doing it or they perceive their peers to be doing it. This activity creates lots of food for thought.

Define peer influence, and see if pupils can think of any examples of it (for example, following fashion, watching a TV programme you don't really like just to fit in with others).

Explain that pupils are going to carry out an experiment to show how powerful peer influence is. The experiment involves all of the top year in school tucking the bottoms of their trousers into their socks for a few days. When any younger pupils ask what is happening, the older pupils are to say, 'this is the cool way to wear your trousers now'. It must be stressed that the success of the experiment relies upon everyone taking part and nobody giving the game away!

After several days, there will almost definitely be an increase in the number of younger children tucking their trousers into their socks.

Use this result to discuss peer influence and raise pupils' awareness of how powerful it can be and how it can sometimes make us behave in a way we would probably never choose for ourselves.

Teaching tip

Discuss the idea that peer influence can also be a good thing. For example, it can stop adults from drinking and driving – as the 'norm' is perceived to be that most adults will not do this.

Taking it further

At the end of the experiment, it is a good idea to do a whole school assembly covering peer influence.

Bonus idea ★

Another year you could get pupils to roll their trousers or sweatshirt sleeves up.

Go on – do it!

"Young people are more likely to make an unwise choice – like smoking – because they believe everyone else is doing it."

During the teenage years, young people can be prone to peer pressure because of an absolute fear of losing face. Help pupils to recognise peer pressure and how to respond to it.

Ask pupils to imagine a scenario where one young person was trying to persuade another to do something they did not want to do (for example, try a cigarette, tease someone, do a criminal dare like shoplifting, etc.). Explain that this is peer pressure. Ask pupils the following questions.

1 Have you ever tried to persuade someone to do something they did not want to do? If so, what?
2 Why do you think some people can be persuaded to do things they clearly don't want to do? (They want to look good in front of their friends; they want to feel 'part of the gang'.)
3 Why do you think one person would try to persuade another person to do something they did not want to do? (This is a difficult question to answer. Perhaps it is a form of teasing, of showing someone up, wanting to get someone into trouble, or enjoying exercising power over someone.)
4 What do you think of a person if they are persuaded? What if they resist? Which person would you respect more?
5 What do you think is the best way to resist being persuaded? (State clearly, 'No, I don't want to', and look like you are not bothered about being pressurised or any response from the other person.)

Taking it further

Explore how advertising can utilise peer pressure. Some adverts even use phrases like 'join the club' or 'do like everyone else'.

Bonus idea ★

Get pupils to role-play a scenario where one person is trying to persuade another to do something risky. Act out one scene where the person is persuaded and another where they are not. Ask which version makes the person being persuaded look best?

Be cool!

"Coolness hierarchies and popularity contests can cause a lot of angst."

Secondary school pupils can be extremely sensitive to criticism from peers for not doing, wearing or saying the right thing. Reflecting upon this tough situation might help pupils to put it into perspective.

Taking it further

Ask pupils to think whether or not they will try to be cool at secondary school. Ask them to give a reason for their answer.

Explain that at secondary school there can be a set of things that make a person 'cool'. These things tend to be superficial and/or unpleasant, for example, smoking, getting lots of likes for photos posted on the internet, having lots of money, teasing other people. Ask pupils if they think these things are cool.

Ask pupils to create a list of attributes that it would be better to have as cool (for example, being kind, making the most of time at school, being confident, being good at a skill, staying true to yourself, appearing not to care what others think about you).

What advice would pupils give to someone who wasn't 'cool' at secondary school; get them to think hard about this.

- Remember the rules of being cool exist much less in the adult world. You will look back and laugh about 'being cool'.
- You can stop the 'cool' thing from being important to you. Focus on things you enjoy. Tell yourself how silly the 'cool' things are. Get on and just be yourself.
- Enjoy your friends.
- Don't spend all evening on social networking sites. Take a break from socialising and the 'cool' nonsense.
- Remember the cool people probably don't feel good about themselves as they cannot be themselves.

Bonus idea ★

Ask pairs of pupils to list what they currently think someone who is 'cool' would be like. Discuss this as a class. Challenge anything that seems superficial. Encourage the idea that really cool is about getting on and being yourself and not worrying too much about what others think of you. Get pupils to create 'truly cool' pictures labelling a person with positive attributes.

The difficult no!

"There can be a lot of guilt attached to saying no."

Learning to be confident to say 'no' when you want or need to is a skill few have. Before we can say no, we need to look at why it is so hard and consider some guidelines that will help make it easier.

Ask pupils to think of a time when they said 'yes' when they really wanted to say 'no', for example, when someone asked to borrow something. Make sure pupils choose something that they really could have said no to. Ask pupils:

- What stopped you from saying no?
- What did you fear people would think of you? What are you scared might happen?
- What benefits are there to being able to say no?

Discuss pupils' answers as a class, and share the following guidelines for saying no.

- Your immediate feelings will usually tell you whether you want to say 'yes' or 'no' to a request.
- If you're not sure then ask for some more information so that you know exactly what you are committing yourself to.
- Say 'no' for yourself, rather than making an excuse for why you don't want to do whatever has been asked of you.
- Make it clear that you are refusing the request and not rejecting the person or the friendship.
- When you say 'no' to something you don't want to do, you are saying 'yes' to yourself and your own importance.
- Saying 'no' and surviving the guilt gets easier with practice!

Taking it further

Quite often when we say yes to things we really didn't want to do, we can find ways to sabotage whatever it was! Give examples of this, for example, going along to an event but being obviously miserable throughout it!

Assert yourself

"People are far more likely to be listened to or get what they want if they are assertive rather than aggressive."

Being assertive does not always mean we get what we want, but it does increase the likelihood of a better outcome than being aggressive or just giving up. This scenario teaches pupils what assertive means.

Ask pupils to imagine that pupil A is trying to persuade pupil B to let him copy some maths homework. Share the following possible responses.

- Pupil B lets pupil A copy the homework even though he really didn't want to. (Passive response)
- Pupil B becomes aggressive and starts insulting pupil A. (Aggressive response)
- Pupil B looks directly at pupil A and states calmly, 'I do not want to give you my homework and I am not going to.' (Assertive response)

Ask pupils to work in pairs and try out all of the responses. With each response ask how the pupils are likely to end up feeling.

- With a passive response pupil B will have given in. Pupil B is unlikely to feel good about this because they have been made to do something they did not want to do. This could make them prone to being persuaded to do more things that they don't want to do.
- With an aggressive response, pupil A might end up also becoming aggressive and a conflict is likely to occur.
- An assertive response means pupil B does not give in but he also shows respect to pupil A. It appears free from emotion and therefore does not open up the person to being teased.

In my humble opinion...

"Having opinions is great, but respecting others' right to hold different ones is something some people need to learn."

Respecting others' opinions is part of growing up! Get pupils to share some opinions with the sole aim of helping them to respect the right of others to hold different opinions.

Set up an agreement spectrum in the room – an imaginary line where one end represents 'strongly agree' and the other end 'strongly disagree'. Make some statements (such as those in the online resources) and ask pupils to stand on the imaginary line in the place that represents how they feel about the statement. (If there is limited space available, devise other ways of letting pupils demonstrate their views such as pointing, raising their hand or using 'agree', 'disagree' or 'neutral' cards.)

Some of these statements will hopefully divide opinion. When pupils have settled into position, ask, 'Who would like to say anything about where they have stood?' Encourage pupils to explain their opinions and debate each issue. Allow them to change position after each debate if they wish. With all opinions aired, regularly:

- Point out that it is OK to hold different opinions.
- State that it is good to be able to back up your opinions with reasons.
- Explain that you need to respect people's right to hold different opinions as long as they do not impact negatively on the rights of others (for example, racism).
- Declare that it is also good to change opinion if you learn something about it that challenges what you knew before.

Taking it further

Ask two confident pupils with opposing views to state their opinions about a topic and their reasons for their opinions. Explore how each pupil feels about someone else having a different opinion. Why do we like it when people agree with us? What is interesting about a person holding a different view? When do we learn more – when someone agrees with us or when they disagree with us?

Quality friendships

"People value different things about their friendships and individual friends 'give' us different things."

Help pupils to reflect upon what makes a quality friendship so they can exercise some discernment in the turbulent teenage years.

Taking it further

Look on the internet for quotes about friendships and discuss the wisdom or learning each one is trying to deliver.

Give pupils the following 'good friend' statements and ask them to sort them from the most to the least important. Discuss each statement before pupils complete an ordering activity. Ask questions like: What do we mean when we say we trust someone? If a friend wants us to do well, what does this mean? In what way might it be important for a friend to notice how we are feeling? In what ways do friends show that they care? What does forgiveness mean?

A good friend:

- is someone you can trust
- is fun and interesting to be with
- always wants you to do well
- pays attention and knows how you are feeling
- makes it clear that they care about you
- stays your friend through both good and bad times
- forgives you when you make mistakes
- is someone you can talk to about almost anything.
- keeps your secrets safe.

Finally ask pupils to complete the sentence start:

- For me, a good friend . . .

Display pupils' responses for all to read. Hopefully it will highlight that different people value different things about friendships.

Bonus idea ★

Ask pupils to make a list of things that damage friendships, which will include things that are the opposite of 'a good friend'. Take the discussion further and ask what needs to happen to repair a damaged friendship.

Friends and feelings

"The key adults in our lives take more of a backseat role and friends step up!"

How well our friendships are going has an impact on how happy we are. This activity helps pupils understand the significance of friends.

Ask each pupil to select two statements from the following that are true for them, and one that is not true for them.

- I feel bad when I fall out with a friend.
- I forgive friends who mess up.
- I am aware that I have hurt friends' feelings in the past.
- I understand that everyone makes friendship mistakes.
- I think a few close friends are better than loads of friends I don't know very well.
- I like to have lots of different friends that I can spend time with.
- I like making new friends.
- I have fallen out with friends in the past and never forgiven them.
- Friends sometimes make me feel good and sometimes make me feel bad.
- I have had the same friends for a long time and this is important to me.
- I can describe a way that I make my friends feel good.
- At secondary school I will spend more time with my friends and they will be even more important to me than they are now.
- I think I am good at keeping friends.
- I have friends I can rely upon to cheer me up.

Ask pupils to find a partner and tell them about the statements they chose and why they chose them. As a class, discuss: how can we make the most of our friends so our friends help us to feel good?

Teaching tip

This activity is a good one to follow Idea 80 – Quality friendships.

Taking it further

Discuss the fact that friends do sometimes mess up. Consider how everyone makes mistakes and that they can be forgiven if they genuinely feel sorry for the upset they have caused and wish to learn from their mistakes. Forgiving someone also releases you from the hurt a person has caused.

Problem page

"Overcoming problems can make a friendship stronger."

Few friendships are completely without difficulties. Help pupils to recognise some common friendship troubles by getting them to give advice to a friends problem page.

Use the following problems, or make up some that have been real difficulties with friendships in your class. Ask groups of pupils to discuss each problem and work out how they would respond.

- My friend is being bullied. If I stick up for him, or if I tell the teacher, the bullies might pick on me. What can I do?
- I fell out with a good friend because another friend told me that she had said I was boring. What can I do?
- I feel jealous of my friend because she seems to be good at everything and everyone likes her. What can I do?
- My best friend is spending more time with someone else than me. I feel like s/he hasn't got time for me anymore. What can I do?
- A group of friends have started teasing me. They think it is funny but it actually upsets me. What can I do?
- My friend keeps trying to persuade me to do things I don't want to do. What can I do?
- My friend only seems to spend time with me when I am happy. If I feel worried or sad about something s/he doesn't want to know, and yet I often support her/him when s/he feels sad. What can I do?

Give pairs of pupils some time to discuss the problems. Next, take the problems one at a time and develop some advice as a class.

Trustworthy?

"Friends that you trust are the ones that help you through difficult times."

Trust is a key element of a healthy relationship but what, exactly, does it mean? Explore the impact of trust and absence of trust on different relationships.

Start by defining trusting relationships, for example, a trusting relationship is one where both people can be relied upon to be honest and do what they say they are going to do.

- Ask pupils to think of someone they really trust. Ask them to write down why they trust this person (for example, they always do what they say they are going to do, they never say one thing to one person and something different to someone else, they can be relied upon to always help).
- Ask pupils to think of someone who probably trusts them. What is it that makes each pupil think this?
- Ask pupils to list how a trustworthy person behaves. What kind of things could a person do that would mean you no longer trusted them?

Next explore how trust impacts on relationships.

- If your parents/carers do not trust you, will they let you do what you like or are they likely to restrict you?
- If a teacher does not trust you to do the right thing, how might this affect how the teacher treats you?
- If you don't trust a friend, what would it stop you from doing with them?

Taking it further

Explain to pupils that as they navigate the secondary school years, friends that they trust will be the ones they rely upon if they ever find themselves having difficulties. Always be grateful for the friends you can trust. Ask pupils to list three friends they really trust.

Bonus idea ★

There are lots of quotes about friendship and trust that can be found on the internet. These can be used to explore the issue of trust further.

To date or not to date

"There can be pressure on teenagers to find a girlfriend or a boyfriend and they might start dating for all the wrong reasons."

Few adults talk to children and young people about 'healthy dating' and yet it can cause a lot of anxiety and confusion. Consider some good dating advice and then get pupils to present it in a way that they think will be interesting for teenagers.

Ask pupils to work in pairs. Explain to pupils that some advice on dating has been written for a teenage magazine and that pupils have been asked to design the page that will include this advice. Explain that pupils will need to:

- give the page a title
- make the page interesting to look at
- include pictures
- write the advice in a way that they think would appeal to teenagers
- give each piece of advice a subtitle.

Give pupils the following advice that is to be included in the article. Ask pupils to take notes as you want them to include all the advice, but to use their own words – words that teenagers will approve of. (You could give low ability pupils a written copy of the advice.)

- Listen to your inner voice to decide whether you want to go out with a particular person. It's usually right and it knows when you feel uncomfortable.
- Be sure you are ready. If you have any doubt – don't start dating.
- Never start dating just because you want to be able to say you have a boyfriend or girlfriend to your peers.
- Talk to friends and parents/carers about what's going on when you are considering dating someone. Seek advice about dating.

- When you date someone, never be pressurised into doing something you do not want to do. 'No' always means 'no'; you can say it in healthy relationships and it will be respected.
- Don't take the relationship too seriously and certainly not at first. You are unlikely to meet your life partner when you are a teenager.
- Remember to give your friends time too and not spend all your spare time with your boyfriend/girlfriend. If the relationship breaks up you need your friends to still be there for you.
- Do a regular happiness check. Does the relationship make you feel good? Are you having fun?
- Do a respect check. Are you being put down or made to feel miserable? Do you feel respected? If not – end it.
- If adults don't take your worries about dating seriously, remind them how intense their feelings were about relationships when they were teenagers and how real those feelings were at the time!

Involving parents

Tell pupils to ask the adult/s at home for their advice about teenage relationships. Ask pupils to write down the piece of advice they believe was the best and bring it into school. Collect in and select a variety of pieces of advice. Share these with pupils and ask them, 'What is good about this piece of advice?'

Body safety

"Every child and young person needs to know that if anyone touches them in a way they don't like or that makes them feel uncomfortable, then they have the right to make it stop."

Pupils should have been made aware of their right to stop any touching, staring or infringements of their privacy long before they reach the end of primary school. However, it is a very important lesson and revising it can only be a good thing before they enter into secondary school. Reiterate this important message.

Teaching tip

Explain to pupils that you should always ask permission before you touch another person. This becomes more and more true as people get older. Some people never like to be touched. Explain that the least threatening place to touch someone to give them reassurance is on the upper arm.

Taking it further

Some parents/carers are slow to realise that their child needs more privacy as he or she grows up. Discuss with pupils the best way of letting a parent/carer know that they need more privacy and discuss exactly what this privacy would actually mean (for example, knocking on the door, a lock on the bathroom door).

To clarify the rights pupils have over their own bodies, state the following:

Nobody should make children or young people do anything they feel uncomfortable with. You have the right to say no to any type of touching – whoever is doing it. This can include touch that hurts, hugging, kissing and any other type of touch. If anyone touches you in a way you do not like, you need to tell them to stop. If they do not stop, you need to find someone who you trust and tell them what is happening. You do not need to keep it a secret even if the person who touched you or touches you tells you that you have to.

As you grow up, you will want more privacy and you are entitled to it. If someone is making you feel uncomfortable by coming into your room without knocking, staring at you in a way that makes you feel uncomfortable or watching you get changed, you need to assertively tell them not to do this. If a situation continues after you have tried to stop it, then you must keep telling trusted adults until someone does something that helps.

Terminate the teasing

"Teasing can seem harmless enough, but sometimes it can hit a nerve and really upset someone."

Everyone has issues they are sensitive about and we cannot always know what these are. Equip pupils with an understanding of how to deal with teasing.

Give pupils some examples of teasing:

- You always look silly when you run.
- I think your shoes look like a clown's.
- You can't spell anything right.

Explain that sometimes teasing can make us laugh and sometimes it can really upset us. Our response to teasing depends upon:

- whether the teasing touches on something we feel sensitive about (the teaser might not know this is a sensitive topic)
- our mood at the time of teasing
- the relationship we have with the person doing the teasing.

Put pupils in pairs and ask them to take it in turns to pretend to tease the other person. Ask the person being teased to respond in four different ways:

- get upset or angry
- tease the person back
- say nothing and put up with the teasing
- agree with the teasing as if it were no big deal, for example, say with a calm voice, 'Yes I know I have a ridiculous run. Funny isn't it?' (This is called fogging.)

Ask pupils which response is most likely to stop a person from teasing you again. They will almost all agree the last response (fogging) has a good chance of preventing further teasing. It is a great response to learn and remember.

Teaching tip

Fogging is best done with no show of emotion. The fact that the teasing appears not to have bothered you in any way makes it boring for the person doing the teasing. It also makes the person being teased look 'cool'.

Taking it further

Show pupils the 'reaction to teasing' flowchart from the online resources. Discuss the scenario of a good friend teasing you. They mean to be funny and they do not realise it is upsetting you. Ask pupils what they think will be the best response in this case. (Tell the friend. If they are a good friend they will be sad to know they have upset you. Honesty from you should make the teasing stop.)

Networking socially

"We have yet to see the long-term impact of social networking on society!"

Hold a discussion with pupils about social networking so they can reflect upon how they will choose to use it in the future.

Explore pupils' understanding of social networks and how they are used. Ask what social networks they have heard of and how people use them. Address any inaccuracies. Next, share the following advice:

- What you post on the internet will give you a reputation. As a rule, if your grandma wouldn't like it, don't post it!
- Be careful about posting your private thoughts. Comments on what you wrote might upset you.
- If you don't trust someone, adjust your privacy settings so they don't see your posts.
- If someone you don't know well offends or upsets you regularly, block them.
- If a good friend posts something that you do not like, be honest and tell them.
- Never post something that you would not say to someone's face. Aim to only say kind things on social network sites.
- Never post your location, phone number or address.
- It's easy to spend a lot of time on social networks. Watch the clock and ensure you get time away from the computer.
- If social networks do not make you feel good, get away from them.
- Always ask permission before posting photos of other people.
- Never tell anyone your password.

Next hold a debate: social networks – are they a good or a bad thing?

Supporting parents and carers

Part 7

A transition evening

"Parents need information and some pointers about how to support their children with the move to secondary school."

Secondary schools usually hold a practical information evening for parents/carers. Enhance this by delivering an evening to support parents/carers with their child's transition to secondary school in a more pastoral role.

Teaching tip

Aim to hold your evening prior to anything offered by the secondary schools so that parents and carers are better equipped to ask questions that will provide helpful answers at the secondary evening.

Be aware of the information parents will receive from any secondary school transition evening and aim to complement it. You could make the primary school evening distinct from the secondary one by calling it something like, 'The challenges of changing school and growing up'.

An evening that aims to help pupils and parents/carers with the transition to secondary school could include many of the ideas included in this book. A typical evening could include:

- Helping your child to deal with the changes involved in the move to secondary school.
- Helping you to understand what will change and the impact this will have on your child.
- Supporting your child to get organised and develop good homework habits.
- How to support your child's learning.
- How to keep in touch with your child's learning and progress.
- Methods for keeping the lines of communication with your child open.
- Some information about anti-bullying.
- The role of mentors.
- A question and answer session.
- Exploring your hopes and dreams for your child's future.

What do you want to know?

"As with anything new, you tend not to be aware of what you don't know and therefore don't know what to ask!"

Help parents/carers to optimise their use of practical information evenings from secondary schools by facilitating the questions that will allay anxieties, prevent misunderstandings and leave parents/carers with a clear idea of the expectations of secondary school life.

To start parents and carers thinking about what will be involved with their child's move to secondary school and the information they might need:

- Send home a questionnaire that invites parents/carers to ask questions about the topics below.
- At a meeting for parents/carers, write the topics below in the centre of flipchart paper and invite them to write on their questions about the issues (they could use sticky notes).
- Set 'homework' where pupils consider the topics below with an adult at home and write down the questions they have.

Topics include:

- homework
- a bigger school
- teachers
- bullying
- variety of subjects
- lunchtime
- school uniform and PE kit
- help at secondary school
- getting to school
- friends
- different sets and groups for lessons
- equipment
- registration
- assemblies.

Taking it further

You could collate the questions and pass them onto the secondary school to inform them of what parents and carers are concerned about so they include this in their session with parents and carers.

Bonus idea ★

In consultation with the secondary school/s produce a FAQs sheet for parents/carers using the most pressing questions raised by this activity.

How can parents help?

"Parents can be made to feel better if they can support their child emotionally and in practical ways."

Parents have a key role in helping their child feel comfortable about the move to secondary school. Give them a comprehensive list of the ways they can support their child with the move.

Emotional support

- Stay positive. Even if you are nervous, try to be excited and upbeat about the move.
- Keep communicating and show an interest once your child starts at secondary school. Ask about school work, new friends, what happens at lunchtime, etc. (Also see Idea 97 – Lines of communication.)
- Look at the school's website with your child.
- Teach your child how to relax – breathing deeply, quiet time before bed (see Idea 70 – And relax. . .).
- Make sure your child is aware of the adults that are in their new school that have a pastoral support role.
- Reassure your child about the common anxieties. Explain that they will soon know their way around their new school, that bullying is rare and that homework will be manageable.
- Share positive stories of your own transition to secondary school.
- Remind your child that not everything changes. Home life will stay the same.
- Make sure your child gets enough sleep.

Taking it further

You could ask pupils what they think their parents/carers could do that would help them with the move to secondary school.

Practical support

- Do a dummy run of the route to school.
- Encourage your child to meet up with friends and walk to school together.
- Make sure your child has the correct school uniform, PE kit and any other equipment they need. Some children get quite anxious about this.
- Make sure your child has a suitably big and durable school bag as they will be carrying more around with them than they did at primary school.
- Encourage your child to develop a morning routine and set their alarm clock so they have plenty of time to complete the routine.
- Create a homework station (see Idea 91 – Parents supporting homework).
- Clarify what your child will have for lunch and how they will get it.
- Encourage your child to pack their bag the night before each school day and check they have responded to any requests or letters from school and that they have all they need – including homework of course.

Bonus idea ★

You could develop a list of ways parents and carers could support their child with the move to secondary school as an activity with parents. This could be done at a parents' evening with ideas being shared there and then. Simply ask groups of parents to create a list of things they could do to help their child, and share the contents of each list with the whole group. Parents will undoubtedly think of things that have not been included on this page.

Parents supporting homework

"Homework is the child's responsibility but parents can nudge them into good habits."

Parents can be key in helping their child to develop good homework habits and you can let them know how.

- Set some rules about when, where and how homework will be completed.
- Encourage your child to get into a routine when they get home from school, for example, a short break with a snack and then an hour of homework.
- Ensure that your child has a place where they can complete homework without being disturbed.
- Some children work well in silence, others can work well with background music. Investigate which genuinely works best for your child.
- Create a homework station – a labelled box full of everything your child might need to complete his or her homework.
- Show an interest in your child's homework.
- If your child is struggling with homework, try and find out the specific cause of the difficulty and then attempt to address it, for example, 'It's too difficult/easy, I find it hard to get started, I don't try hard with it – I just want to get it done, it's taking too long, I forget what I am meant to do, I get distracted'.
- If your child consistently has difficulties, contact the school and see if some solutions can be worked out or a teacher can provide appropriate support.

Independent organisation

"Being organised is a valuable skill for life."

Pupils will need to take responsibility for their own organisation, but a helping hand from parents can support this.

Responsibilities at secondary school include:

- organising homework – completing it and handing it in on time
- wearing the correct school uniform
- making sure to have a PE kit on PE days
- making sure to have the correct equipment for lessons and other activities
- getting to school on time
- relaying key messages about school to parents/carers and ensuring any requirements are met
- making sure to have their lunch or provision for it and making sure to eat it
- getting to different lessons on time
- knowing where to go for occasional needs, such as medical or lost property.

Ask parents how they could help their children to get organised about these things and introduce the advice below.

- Construct a 'what you need on each day' timetable.
- Put reminders on the front door for lunch money, homework, PE kit, etc.
- Create a homework wall chart that your child can write on.
- Ask 'Is there anything different or special you need to remember to do this week?' on a Sunday night.
- Encourage children to pack their school bag in the evening ready for the next day.
- Give regular praise for good organisation.
- Discuss the hazards of getting distracted.

> **Teaching tip**
>
> Some children are naturally better at organising themselves than others. Ultimately the aim is to get pupils organising themselves independently. Many teenagers want to be trusted to get themselves organised and start to resent parents even reminding them what to do. This is why subtle reminders can be more effective than constant ones! Discuss this with parents and carers.

All about the learning

"Showing an interest in your child's learning can be very motivational for them."

Give parents/carers some tips about how they can help their child engage with the curriculum and maintain motivation.

- Show an enthusiastic interest in their homework. Offer to read it through.
- Ask about different subjects. Which ones do they like best? Which do they struggle with? What do they like about the subjects they enjoy?
- Ask your child which topics they are studying, for example, in history. Use the internet or books to find out about the topics and discuss anything interesting you find.
- If your child is struggling in a subject, there are plenty of revision guides available. You could offer to learn alongside your child.
- Find learning games online to support the subjects your child is covering.
- Be a good role model – demonstrate and declare how much you enjoy learning.
- Explore the ways your child prefers to learn. What really helps them to take information in? Try out some of the methods from Idea 68 – Learning how to learn.
- Contact the school if your child is struggling with a particular subject; see whether the subject teacher can offer any advice.
- Many secondary schools document each pupil's progress via the school's website, usually in a 'zone' for parents/carers. Check this regularly and comment on progress; praise good progress and offer support for poor progress.

Bonus idea ★

Introduce parents/carers to the preferences for visual, auditory and kinaesthetic learning. Ask them to complete a test (type VAK test into a search engine). This demonstrates to parents/carers that we all have different learning preferences.

Find a mentor

"You don't want your children to be completely dependent on you for the rest of your lives!"

Help parents and carers to recognise that adult mentors can be positive role models who can help guide their children through their teenage years, and consider where to find them.

Explain to parents/carers that finding a mentor for a child can be beneficial, especially for the teenage years. An ideal mentor will be someone the child has known for a while, but this is not mandatory. A good mentor might be an aunt or uncle, the leader of a club, a sports or music teacher, a neighbour, a friend's parent, or the parent's close friend.

Discuss the idea of mentors with parents. Ask:

- What is a mentor? (Somebody who can provide guidance, advice and support.)
- What are the qualities of a good mentor? (Accessible, non-judgemental, a good listener.)
- In what ways would you expect a mentor to help your child? (Provide an alternative 'ear', give advice, help them when they struggle, be someone who they can share things with.)
- In what way would a mentor be helpful particularly when your child goes through the teenage years? (A mentor will give them a trusted adult who they are willing to turn to for help.)
- Do you (the parents/carers) remember having any mentors in your teenage years? How did they help?
- Which adults that you know might be good mentors for your child?

Teaching tip

Some parents/carers might struggle with the idea that their child will get to a point where they are reluctant to ask them for help. Stress that this is a normal and healthy part of growing up and a shift towards greater independence.

Hopes and dreams

"Few pupils know what they want to do in the future when they are at primary school."

Exploring pupils' future aspirations alongside their parents can be an engaging, positive and motivational activity. Add this activity to any transition evening you deliver for parents and carers.

This activity goes well with Idea 27 – Aspirations!, which looks at the links between what a child might do well with at school and possible future careers. You can instigate a more general discussion about pupils' futures in the following way.

Give parents/carers the following list (either on a sheet or on a flipchart):

- learn to drive
- go to university or college
- have children
- get a well-paid job
- get a job you really enjoy
- find a life partner you are happy with
- have some really good friends
- find things you really enjoy doing
- travel and see other countries
- be fit and healthy
- be a kind adult.

Ask pupils and parents/carers to think separately of how important each of these things would be. Ask both the child and the parents to mark each thing out of ten for importance.

Ask the parents/carers and their children to take one item at a time and share with each other the scores they gave it.

Ask parents and their children to explain the scores they gave. This usually leads to a considerable amount of discussion.

Taking it further

Ask pupils to write a list of three ambitions for their future (for example, travel to a particular place, learn something like a language or to play a musical instrument, get a particular career, have children). Give these to the parents to keep in a safe place and look at in years to come!

Call school

"There are some things for which contacting the school is the best thing to do."

Primary school teachers and staff can seem more accessible to parents and carers than secondary school staff. Help parents/carers to understand that although secondary school is different they can still make contact, and in some cases it is vital that they do so.

Parents and carers will probably be given contact details when they attend any secondary transition evening, but it cannot hurt for you to make clear:

1 the different ways in which a parent can contact the school (usually phone and email)
2 that different numbers are usually used for different types of contact, for example absence can be a different telephone number to the one used for a pastoral care issue.

Also make clear the reasons why a secondary school would expect a parent to make contact. For example:

- absence – this usually has to be reported by telephone on the morning of absence
- changes in details (for example, a change in address)
- to give medical information that a school might need to know (for example, allergies, a diagnosis of diabetes or epilepsy)
- when a child is having difficulties in a particular subject or with homework
- if you suspect your child is being bullied (the school should take this very seriously and respond quickly)
- any circumstances that might impact on your child's well-being and ability to focus (for example, bereavement, parents separating).

Taking it further

Find out and share with parents/carers how the secondary school keeps parents informed (for example, newsletters, emails, information about individual pupils on their website) and any reasons that they are likely to contact them (for example, unauthorised absences, behaviour problems, sudden drops in academic marks).

Lines of communication

"Some children share readily, others share very little."

Inform parents of ways in which they can try and keep lines of communication open with their child throughout the teenage years.

Teaching tip

There are many books written about how to cope as a parent of a teenager. Collect a list of books that get good reviews to share with parents.

Taking it further

There are stories of very one-sided communication between parents and their teenage children. One such story tells of a parent who wrote her son little notes every day and put them under his pillow. She wasn't even sure if he was reading them. Years later, when the son was in his twenties, he told his mother that sometimes, when he felt really bad, it was only her notes that 'saved' him from complete despair. Share this story to parents to illustrate that even if there is no response, it doesn't mean there isn't any positive impact!

Parents can find their child's teenage years difficult to navigate, and communication is not usually as straightforward as it was when their child was at primary school. Some teenagers can seem very reluctant to share any information, but this might not mean that they want their parents to stop communicating altogether – it can just mean that the methods need to change.

Share some simple ideas that can help keep parents a little informed about what is going on in their child's life and to keep communication happening – even if it is not direct. For example:

- Give your child a notebook and explain that you will use it to write to them now and then. Explain that they can use it to tell you things too. Promise to respond to anything they write in it.
- Write your child little notes telling them positive things you have noticed about them and leave them in their room.
- When your child has friends round, ask them questions about school and what's been happening. They might tell you more than your child does – and more than they tell their own parents!
- Keeping communication brief can work well. Ask your child for a quick mark out of ten for how good their day has been.
- Try not to communicate with your child when either of you are angry or upset.

Protect or equip

"Some parents metaphorically wrap their children in cotton wool."

This activity helps parents come to terms with their child's growing need for independence. It can sometimes result in epiphanies!

Define equipping and protecting in the following way for parents/carers.

- Equipping: teaching your child how to keep themselves safe.
- Protecting: keeping your child away from any potential dangers.

Print these actions on flash cards and share them with parents/carers. Ask them to sort them into piles: one for 'equipping' (E) and one for 'protecting' (P).

- Never letting your 16-year-old go to a party. (P)
- Talking to your 14-year-old about how alcohol affects you. (E)
- Teaching your six-year-old child to cross the road safely. (E)
- Stopping your four-year-old from seeing violence on the TV. (P)
- Telling your nine-year-old you have never smoked when you have. (P)
- Discussing reasons for and consequences of smoking with your nine-year-old. (E)
- Teaching your three-year-old not to touch something hot. (E)
- Keeping medicines in a cupboard out of the reach of your four-year-old. (P)
- Telling your fifteen-year-old never to drink alcohol. (P)
- Talking to your sixteen-year-old about safer sex. (E)
- Putting safety covers on plug sockets to stop your one-year-old from putting their fingers in them. (P)

Teaching tip

With 'protect' and 'equip' as they are defined here, share with parents: it is appropriate to protect children from things they cannot yet be equipped to protect themselves from (for example, a one-year-old with plug sockets); as a parent/carer we should aim to equip our children and then trust them to go safely on their own.

Taking it further

To start up a discussion ask parents:

- Is protecting more appropriate for younger or older children?
- If we ultimately cannot be with our children all the time for the rest of their lives, does equipping or protecting make more sense with teenagers?
- Some parents protect their children for longer than others – as a parent do you think you have encouraged your child to make safe choices independently of you?

Signs of bullying

"Some children blame themselves for being bullied."

Because not all pupils tell, it is important that parents and carers are aware of the signs they might see in their child that could indicate that s/he is being bullied.

Before you share the following list of signs that might indicate that a child is being bullied, emphasise that you are sharing the list because you think it's good for parents to have this information, not because you think the secondary school has a bullying problem!

Signs that indicate that your child might be being bullied:

- a sudden drop in school marks
- unexplained bruises, cuts or injuries
- broken or missing possessions, for example, phone, bag, clothing
- does not want to go to school – might feign illness
- does not want to see peers – even at activities outside school that they enjoy
- a tendency to want to be on his or her own
- physical complaints – such as headaches or stomach aches
- signs of stress such as difficulty sleeping
- being really hungry after school – a bully might have taken dinner money
- a significant change in typical behaviour – moody, angry, depressed
- starting to bully younger siblings
- wanting to spend more time with you all of a sudden

Obviously some of these symptoms could have a cause other than bullying.

Taking it further

You could spend more time exploring the topic of anti-bullying if parents/ carers express an interest in you doing so. For this you could adapt several activities in the anti-bullying section of this book.

Goodbye primary school

"Many parents feel attached to their child's primary school."

This activity is a lovely way for pupils to say goodbye to their primary school and to collect fond memories to enjoy when they are older. Parents will enjoy it too.

As a homework project for the final half term, ask pupils to produce a memoir of their time at primary school. This could be produced in a variety of formats including:

- an elaborate and decorated timeline
- a booklet
- a film
- a wall display
- a newspaper.

Pupils could include the following in their memoir.

- A brief fact file on each of their teachers.
- A top five list of primary school memories.
- A plan of the school labelled with memories, for example, the piano where Mrs X played, the PE cupboard full of jumbled hockey sticks in the corner.
- A map of their route to school.
- Particular memories of school events like discos, school trips, school fetes.
- Any memory of their very first day.
- Any lesson that sticks in their mind.

Encourage pupils to involve their parents/ carers, who could provide:

- descriptions of their memory of particular events
- opinions about their child's experiences
- photos of the child from different ages (especially wearing school uniform)
- funny memories of their child at each age.

Taking it further

The best ideas from the memoirs could be collated and put together as a yearbook for the school to keep.

Bonus idea ★

The memoirs could be displayed at a leavers' exhibition as outlined in Idea 16 – Celebrate good times.